OLIVIA ON THE RECORD

A Radical Experiment in Women's Music

OLIVIA ON THE RECORD

A Radical Experiment in Women's Music

Ginny Z Berson

With love for justice —
G Z Berson

aunt lute books
San Francisco

"Freedom Time" used with permission of Linda Tillery; "Hello Hooray" based on the Rolf Kempf song "Hello, Hurray," used with permission; "Leaping" used with permission of Sue Fink; "Don't Pray for Me" and "No Hidin' Place" used with permission of Mary Watkins; "Kahlua Mama" used with permission of Virginia Rubino; "Song to My Mama," "Ode to a Gym Teacher," "Valentine Song," "Rosalind" used with permission of Meg Christian; "Joanna," "If It Weren't for the Music," "Song of the Soul," "Waterfall" used with permission of Cris Williamson; "Carol, in the park, chewing on straws," "Anathema" used with permission of Judy Grahn; "[My Lover Is a Woman]" © Anastasia Dunham-Parker-Brady, 2020. Used with permission.

Album covers for *Lesbian Concentrate* and *The Ways a Woman Can Be*, gift certificate for *I Know You Know*, excerpt from liner notes for *Lesbian Concentrate*, original Olivia Records logo, excerpt from liner notes for *The Ways a Woman Can Be*, excerpt from *I Know You Know Songbook*. All used with permission of Judy Dlugacz.

Cover photo © 2020 JEB (Joan E. Biren)

Aunt Lute Books
P.O. Box 410687
San Francisco, CA 94141
www.auntlute.com

Print ISBN: 9781951874018
ebook ISBN: 9781939904379

Book design and typesetting: A.S. Ikeda
Cover design: Poonam Whabi
Senior Editor: Joan Pinkvoss
Artistic Director: Shay Brawn
Managing Editor: A.S. Ikeda
Production: Maya Sisneros, María Mínguez Arias, Emma Rosenbaum, Calli Storrs

Publication of this book was made possible, in part, by support from the Sara and Two C-Dogs Foundation.

Library of Congress Cataloging-in-Publication Data

Names: Berson, Ginny, author.
Title: Olivia on the record : a radical experiment in women's music /
    Ginny Z Berson.
Description: San Francisco : Aunt Lute Books, [2020]
Identifiers: LCCN 2020024078 (print) | LCCN 2020024079 (ebook) | ISBN
    9781951874018 (paperback) | ISBN 9781939904379 (ebook)
Subjects: LCSH: Olivia Records, Inc. | Sound recording industry--United States--
    History--20th century. | Women's music--History and criticism. | Feminism
    and music--United States.
Classification: LCC ML3792.O55 B47 2020 (print) | LCC ML3792.O55 (ebook)
    | DDC 781.64082/0973--dc23
LC record available at https://lccn.loc.gov/2020024078
LC ebook record available at https://lccn.loc.gov/2020024079

Printed in the U.S.A. on acid-free paper
10 9 8 7 6 5 4 3 2 1

To all who yearn for justice and walk the path of love and compassion.

ACKNOWLEDGMENTS

Olivia operated as a collective, and although this book was not written collectively, it would have been much thinner without our collective memories. Enormous gratitude to the women who answered my pleas for help whenever I called or emailed, always answering my "do you remember this and when was it and who else was there?" and who were so essential to the early days of Olivia—Shambhavi Meg Christian, Kate Winter, Jennifer Woodul, Liz Brown, Sandy Ramsey, Judy Dlugacz. Thanks to all the women who let me interview them to get their sides of things, their experiences, their memories: Linda Tillery, Mary Watkins, Teresa Trull, Robin Flower, Karlene Faith, Sandy Stone, Kim Johnson, Barbara Smith, Diane Sabin, Emily Culpepper, Helaine Harris, Amy Horowitz, and the late great Joan Lowe. And to Cris Williamson for saying the magic words. The analysis and any errors of fact are mine alone.

Coletta Reid, Tasha Singer, Lee Schwing and Jennifer Woodul were helpful to me on The Furies chapter.

For years, my friends Achy Obejas and Torie Osborn leaned on me to write this story and really planted the seed. But before I wrote this book, I didn't know how to write a book. Luckily, Judy Grahn was about to start a memoir-writing class, and I signed up immediately. I thank Judy and the classmates who were so important to the initial drafts—especially Joellen Hiltbrand, and Dianne Jenett.

To the women who read different drafts or chapters and gave me useful feedback, I give thanks: Jackie Dennis, Nancy Berson, Lydia Koza, Sandy Stone, and Shakti Butler. To JoAnn Ugolini and Don Cushman, for good listening on salon nights.

Thanks to Penny Rosenwasser and Judy Werle for invaluable advice and encouragement.

I heard a million stories about how awful publishing is now, how there are no good editors, etc. My experience working with Aunt Lute Books was completely the opposite. This press has been in existence since 1982—a feminist institution—and they have been absolutely wonderful to work with. Joan Pinkvoss should get an award for being such an excellent editor. The book is better because of her editing skills, our shared history, and her willingness always to consider everything. Gratitude to all the Aunt Luters who had anything to do with this—especially Shay Brawn, A.S. Ikeda, and Emma Rosenbaum. I hope everyone who reads this will buy ten books from Aunt Lute. Let's keep them alive and healthy.

Finally, for her endless support, ideas, shoulder rubs, suggestions, encouragement when I was sure the book would never happen, and love, I thank my beloved partner, Jackie Dennis.

Contents

OLIVIA ON THE RECORD

A Radical Experiment in Women's Music

Prologue

I
T's A COLD NIGHT IN December 1977 at the Oakland
Auditorium in Oakland, California. Intermission has ended
and the crowd of two thousand has quieted as the band begins
its set. The band is all women. Everyone working on this show—
the stage manager, lighting designer, sound engineer, sign
language interpreter, promoter, producer, childcare providers,
and the entire crew—is a woman, and at the end of the show,
everyone will be paid. There are two long sets per half, actually
four short sets each. The four short sets are performed by Meg
Christian, Teresa Trull, Pat Parker, and Cris Williamson. The
band is led by Linda Tillery, whose newly released album we are
celebrating. She is backed by Alberta Jackson, Jerene Jackson,
Chris Hansen, Vicki Randle, Diane Lindsay, Colleen Stewart,
and Mary Watkins. It's the second night of this sold-out event.
The first night was billed as "especially for women," but even on
this second night there are far more women than men. Tickets
went for $4.50 and were sold in women's bookstores all over the
Greater Bay Area. The concert is wheelchair accessible, which
is not the norm in 1977.

This was an Olivia Records event and all these women
recorded for Olivia. Olivia Records was a national women's
record company, founded by a group of lesbian feminists in

Washington, DC, in 1973. We were determined to change the music industry, but more than that—much more than that—we were determined to change the world. To overthrow the patriarchy and capitalism. To end racism and imperialism. To create a world where "peace" and "justice" and "equity" were not just words, but were righteous ideas to be embodied inside ourselves and fought for in the world. Feminism was not a laundry list of issues for us. It was a different way to understand and use power—to benefit the whole, not to advantage the few. Yes, we wanted lots of things on that laundry list, and we wanted more. What we did would prove to be important. *How* we did it was just as important.

As I stood in the back of the concert hall on that night in December, I believed that this show—with these Black and white women on stage, with these women of all races and backgrounds working behind the scenes—was another step on the road towards our lesbian feminist revolution.

We had big dreams, some might say ridiculous dreams, in what seemed like very dark and dangerous days—Richard Nixon was stirring up fear and resentment towards Black people, college students, and anyone who didn't agree with him; the war in Vietnam was still raging and thousands were dying; J. Edgar Hoover was using the FBI to infiltrate and help destroy radical political movements like the Black Panther Party and who knew who else. We had a vision that we held on to tightly and expressed constantly in every way we could. We made big mistakes, and we learned from some of them. We kept moving. We had our hearts broken, and we kept going. We were lesbians, and we did the unthinkable—we centered our lives on women.

The story people were told in the 1970s by the government and mainstream media about "Women's Lib," as they insultingly called it, described the movement as a bunch of white, middle-class, suburban women who really just wanted their husbands to help more around the house. But there was a part of the women's movement of the 1970s that was visionary, revolutionary, anti-racist, and very grounded in women's real needs and aspirations. We understood that culture and politics were not separate, that each was informed by the other and, when consciously united, created a much more powerful force for change. We were going for hearts and minds. We did not want a piece of "the pie," which we considered poisoned, contaminated by greed and the need to dominate. We wanted a whole new pie, filled with love and justice and with enough for everybody.

That is the spirit in which we created Olivia Records. This is the spirit behind this musically disjointed concert we produced in 1977. This is the story I am about to tell.

This is my story. There is no "official" story. Every one of us who was there will tell it differently. I spoke to many of the women I mention in this book to try to fill in my own memory gaps, and I was surprised how often the person I was speaking to had a slightly, or even largely, different recollection of what happened, who was there, when it happened, etc. It helped that I saved stuff—decades of appointment books, letters people wrote me, carbon copies of letters I wrote, original documents, drafts of articles. I must have known that someday I would want all of this, and that it would be important.

Nor is Olivia Records the only story. Yes, we were unique in our vision, our intentions, and our approach, but we were not alone. There were lots of women making Women's Music, as we came to call it, and making records in the 1970s. And there were festivals that celebrated Women's Music and culture. Kate Millett organized a festival in Sacramento in 1973. The National Women's Music Festival was originally held on the campus of the University of Illinois at Champaign–Urbana. It started in 1974 and is still going on in various sites in the Midwest. The

Michigan Womyn's Music Festival ended its forty-year run in 2015, in part because of the controversy over its exclusion of trans women. But for the many years I attended (my last year was 1994), it was an extraordinary experience because it was about more than the music—it was about creating community, a city of women, built on feminist principles and values, and in which, for the only time/place in our lives, lesbian culture was the dominant culture.

Olivia played an important role, influencing and inspiring much of what happened—giving voice to women's different realities, providing opportunities for women to learn and practice new skills and then create networks among themselves, building community and recognizing that music would be an important part of that—and we were influenced and inspired by what other women were doing as well. We live again in very dark and dangerous days. What we do every day matters. What we did—all of us—matters. It mattered then and it matters now. I didn't have this language then, but what I wanted—what we wanted—was to be able to be fully ourselves, for *all* women to be able to be our full selves. That is still what I want, and that is why I'm telling this story.

1 The Road I Took

I Could Have Been a Yankee
but Instead I Was a Fury

ON A WARM SPRING DAY, on a dirt field behind the playground at Stratfield School in Fairfield, Connecticut, I am pounding my baseball glove with my right fist, waiting for my 4th grade classmate Gary to come up to the plate. As he does, I move easily into a perfect shortstop crouch—knees bent, leaning with my weight forward, glove slightly off the ground. I would feel better if I weren't wearing a dress, but, in 1956, girls had to wear dresses to school. No matter. Out of the corner of my eye, I see my classmate Warren, the third baseman, take a few steps in towards home plate, and I move a little to my right. Gary has been known to drop a bunt, and Warren is trying to protect against that. But Gary doesn't bunt. He smashes a hard drive down the third base line, over Warren's head. I fly over to my right, reach my glove hand in front of my body, and snag the scorching liner out of the air. Gary is out. I have saved our team at least one run. And I now know for certain that when I grow up I will be playing shortstop for the New York Yankees. What could possibly keep me from my true destiny?

I soon learned the answer to that question. Not only would I not be allowed to play professional baseball, I wouldn't even be allowed to play Little League baseball, and thus were planted the seeds of rebellion that would become revolutionary

For my 10th birthday, I got a New York Yankees
jacket and a Hank Bauer bat. Heaven.

consciousness. All I ever wanted to do was play baseball, and
I was good at it. To be told that I was not allowed to do this
thing that I could do better than most of the boys I knew was
ridiculous. And infuriating. Twenty years later, my career would
peak when I was selected for the Los Angeles Class A Fast
Pitch Lesbian Bar League All-Star Softball Team, representing
Terry's Trumpeteers. I got the only RBI for our team. But back
in the 1950s, I was learning that there were mountains of things
that I wasn't going to be able to do because I was a girl. Like
become a rabbi, or president of the United States, or act on my
attractions towards other girls and women. Were all the rules
this stupid and unfair?

Actually, as it turned out, many of them were. My parents
laid down all kinds of rules that my sisters and I were expected
to follow unquestioningly. When we dared to challenge them,
they usually responded in one of two ways—either "because
I said so" or a smack across the face. I think that helped instill

in me a longing for justice, but not a lot of ambition to question its lack, at least in my family. I watched the brutal response to the Civil Rights Movement unfold on TV, and our rabbi was a Freedom Rider, so I learned something about courage and taking risks for what you believed in from those two sources. I suppose I could have taken the world as it was presented to me and just accepted it—"this is how things are, and you might as well get used to it." Instead, as I experienced and witnessed injustice pile on injustice, something began to grow inside me. I had doubts.

In the fall of 1960, I was fourteen years old, a sophomore in high school. I applied to be our high school's choice for Junior Year Abroad; those selected would live with a family in another country, undoubtedly in Western Europe. I was one of the three finalists, and I was preparing for my interview. The United States and the Soviet Union were at the height of a protracted Cold War, so I knew there would be questions about how I would portray the US to the family and schoolmates in whatever country I was sent to. I thought the United States was the greatest place on earth, notwithstanding the fact that I had never been anywhere else. We had Democracy. We had Freedom. We had Truth. I wasn't at all worried about how I would answer the questions about representing My Country. Then I started thinking that the Russians probably believed that they had the best country in the world too, and they thought that because their government lied to them. And for some reason, I started playing with the idea that our government might be lying to us, and how would we know? I mentioned this in my interview along with the *caveat* that I would never discuss this with people in my host country. It was truly a surprise to me that I was not the chosen one.

≈

A few years later, in 1964, I am a sophomore at Mount Holyoke College, a women's college in South Hadley, Massachusetts. I am standing at the back of the stage of the college amphitheater, one of only eight or ten students chosen to be part of the honor guard for Hubert Humphrey, who is about to arrive. We are all holding red, white, and blue posters with Lyndon Johnson's and Humphrey's faces over the campaign slogan "Johnson–Humphrey for the USA." I am chanting "All the way with LBJ." I have been chosen because I am active in the local Democratic Party, and I think Lyndon Johnson has already been a great president, having taken over after John Kennedy's assassination, and I am thrilled to be here supporting his election bid. My job, along with the other students, is to stand on the stage behind Humphrey, cheer when appropriate, wave my sign enthusiastically, and look adoringly at the vice presidential candidate. I do all of these things with great sincerity.

Two years later, I am a senior, and I am standing outside the college administration building with eight or ten other students in a vigil that we hold every week. The sign I am holding says "Stop the war now," and we are chanting, "Hey, hey, LBJ, how many kids did you kill today?" Almost everyone ignores us, but if any other students do pay attention, it is to tell us they hope it will rain or snow on the day of our vigil. This only makes us more determined to go out no matter how miserable the conditions.

I had been moved to change my position on the war and my perspective on the government by a guy I dated who challenged my support for the war with questions I couldn't answer. I began to wonder once again if our government might be lying to us. I started reading, and then I started questioning, and then I stopped accepting, and then I stopped believing, and through this process I was radicalized. There is a line in "Waterfall," a Cris Williamson song that she hadn't even written yet—"When you open up your life to the living, all things come spilling in on you." That's what happened. I started to see the world very differently, and, although it made no sense to me at all, everything became much clearer. Those seeds of doubt that were first planted on a baseball field were now flowering. I saw connections between the treatment of American Black people and Vietnamese people. I started to understand that poverty was not an accident or symptom of laziness and personal failure. Although I didn't extend these realizations to myself as a woman, I was beginning to recognize systems.

Later in my senior year, in February 1967, Stokely Carmichael, who would take the name Kwame Ture, was invited to speak at the college. Carmichael was one of the leaders of SNCC (Student Nonviolent Coordinating Committee) and is credited with coining the term "Black Power." I don't know who was responsible for inviting him, but Judith, my friend and classmate—one of the four Black students in this first class to have more than one—was asked introduce him and was supposed to direct the Q&A that would follow his speech. Bringing Stokely Carmichael to Mount Holyoke College in the semi-rural asparagus valley of Western Massachusetts was a pretty radical act in and of itself, and it drew lots of attention beyond the college. The closest TV station, from the city of Holyoke, sent a camera crew so they could do a story for the eleven o'clock news. They set up their big camera on a big tripod with their big and very bright lights in the center aisle about twenty feet from the lip of the stage. The auditorium was full, and in her introduction Judith laid out the history of Stokely's involvement in the Civil Rights Movement. A few of us cheered loudly. As he started to speak, the camera started rolling and the TV lights went on. Stokely was blinded by the light; he tried angling his hand so he could see his speech and the audience without looking into the lights, but he couldn't do it. He asked the TV crew to turn out the lights. They refused. Judith got up from her seat to intervene, and she immediately had to shield her eyes. She asked them to cut the lights. They kept filming. Stokley asked again. They refused again. So he walked off the stage, and that was the end of Stokely Carmichael's appearance at Mount Holyoke College.

But that was not the end for us. Some of us—especially the small group that stood every week at the anti-war vigil—were angry and disappointed. We had really wanted to hear him speak. Most of us were in the same dorm (good thing, because we had strictly enforced curfews, the college feeling the need to act in place of our over-protective parents) and we gathered in the common room to watch the eleven o'clock news. The whole story lasted about one minute and only showed Stokely fighting with the lights and walking off the stage. The only reference to what he stood for was a smirking mention of "Black Power" as if it were a disease.

Now we were really angry and started calling the TV station to register our complaint. After three or four of us got through, they stopped answering the phone. But we were still not finished.

First thing the next morning, we met again and decided to go to the TV station and demand a meeting with the station manager. Four of us drove into Holyoke and marched into the station. After a short wait, we were shown into the station manager's office. He had several TV monitors running, all with the sound off. He told us that the station should have run a bit more about Stokely's message and shouldn't have made the whole story about his inability to see past the lights. But, he said, that was yesterday's news, and there was nothing to be done now. At which point we saw on one of the monitors that the station was re-running the exact same clip and story as part of their morning newscast.

Caught with his proverbial pants down, the manager apologized and asked us what he could do about it now, since Stokely was long gone from the area. We asked him to send a crew to Mount Holyoke and interview students—ask us what we thought Stokely's message was and what we thought of it. He agreed, but said that he would want to interview students regardless of their viewpoints. No problem, we said, and raced back to campus to get the word out to as many like-minded people as we could.

And so the evening news that night ran a story with four or five white Mount Holyoke students, of whom I was one, talking about why we supported Black Power.

I was beginning to understand that even a small group of people working together could make things happen. I was experiencing the thrill of women in concert, operating without authoritarian leadership or formal structure, having an impact. Making change.

When my politics began to change, I noticed a growing distance between my friends and me, as I kept trying to change the subject from boys we were dating or wishing we were dating to news of the war and the anti-war movement. I didn't want to drink beer with them and make up stories about how and when I had lost my virginity—something which apparently everyone but me had done years ago. I started hanging out with the women who stood every week in the anti-war vigil, the same women who did the Stokely Carmichael action. When we drank beer we talked about Ho Chi Minh and Che Guevara and debated the politics of Malcolm X versus Martin Luther King, and we listened to Simon and Garfunkel singing "Sounds of Silence" and Phil Ochs singing "Ringing of Revolution." We did not talk about boys.

I didn't know why the other women avoided the subject, but it was perfectly fine with me. I had known I was a lesbian before I even knew the word for what I was feeling. I didn't discuss it with anybody and hoped that it would just go away. I had heard people say the word "dyke" to describe girls and women who were considered completely unattractive, mentally ill, and sub-human. Who would want to be that? So I dated boys in high school and men in college and tried to like it, but I always preferred the company of my female friends. I had big crushes on lots of women and wrangled ways to be around them while always pretending that I could take them or leave them. The story I told myself was that I was too cool to really care. But I did care, and every time I spent even an hour with one of my crushes, I left feeling somewhat concerned about my attraction but also buzzing with new energy for my fantasies.

I graduated in June 1967 with a degree in political science, a huge amount of anger at the US government, a deep sense of frustration that we were unable to stop the war, a lot of debt, and a desire to become a community organizer and work with Saul Alinsky, the founder of modern community organizing. But to work with Alinsky in 1967, you either had to have organizing experience or you had to attend his training, which was not cheap. I had no experience and no money. So I decided to join the Peace Corps. This would address so many of my issues—I would get organizing experience; I would get my college debt deferred while I was serving; I would get to travel to Latin America, a place I felt very drawn to; I would get out of the US before my growing rage exploded. I understood that the Peace Corps was just another tool of US foreign policy, which I already identified as imperialistic, but it had a kinder face, and I thought I might be of service to the people of the country I was assigned to.

For two years, from 1967–1969, I lived in Río Abajo, a barrio in Panama City, learned how to organize people, helped folks make some small changes in the neighborhood, became fluent in Spanish, made life-long friends, smoked enormous quantities of dope, began to understand the meaning of class privilege, played shortstop on the local Pinturas Glidden softball team, lived through a coup, and almost quit fifty times because of my discomfort with the contradictions I was living.

The Pinturas Glidden softball team in Panama City.

I also came out to a fellow Peace Corps Volunteer (PCV) named Roger, who was gay and who knew immediately upon meeting me that I was too. Roger and I believed what we had been taught our whole lives directly and indirectly, whether it was named or whether it was not named—that our attraction to people of the same gender was not normal. It was disgusting. It was a sickness. But Roger convinced me that we could cure ourselves. I was desperate to do so. I would have given anything to be rid of my feelings for women.

I developed a plan and proceeded to follow it. I had my hair straightened (for some reason, I thought having wildly curly hair made it obvious that I was a lesbian), got some new dresses and skirts (women in Panama in the late 1960s never wore pants in public), and found a new PCV who had just arrived in Panama and didn't know the old me. He was engaged to a woman in the States, which may explain why I was willing to get involved with him. I also liked him. We had a good time together, a lot of which was spent stoned, and we had decent sex. But I never felt attracted to him, and, when he left Panama after a few months, I knew that my experiment with heterosexuality was over. And though I had no intention of acting on my feelings for women, I was almost ready to accept that they weren't going away.

At the end of my two-year stint in Panama, in August 1969, I shipped home bags of marijuana hidden inside the middle of books whose pages I had removed, and I rescued my friend Ronnie—who was as ready to come home as I was—from having to spend an extra month in the country. Ronnie was a PCV assigned to Pan de Azúcar, another barrio of Panama City, and we had become best friends two years earlier during Peace Corps training. She actually saved me first. Before being sent to Panama, our group had gathered in Philadelphia for language testing and a series of vaccines. I had an almost pathological fear of getting shots, and, on my second day in Philly, I had to get three. I was sitting in the lobby of the hotel where they put us up, practically shaking, when I saw a familiar face saunter by.

"Are you Ronnie?" I asked somewhat meekly.

"That's me," she replied coming over to sit by me. "I'm sorry, I don't remember your name. You are…"

"Terrified of needles. Oh, I'm Ginny. Are you going to get your shots?"

She said she was. I asked if I could go with her. She said of course, that having company would make getting stuck with needles more tolerable. And we have been friends ever since.

With our two years almost up, we were both so ready to come home, counting the remaining days from about six months out, dreaming about hot showers and cool weather and a cockroach-free environment. We had to pass a physical before we could leave, and that included checking for parasites. That meant shitting in a cup three days in a row, putting the cup in a paper bag, walking the quarter mile to the bus stop, and taking a thirty-minute bus ride to the lab in downtown Panama City. Panama is a tropical country, and it's very hot and humid, even in winter, but this was August. The buses were small, crowded, and not air-conditioned, and it was hard not to think that everybody could tell from the smell what was in my little brown paper bag.

I had no parasites. Alas, Ronnie did. She would have to stay in Panama for at least another month. Even though Ronnie's home was in Manhattan, which housed a center for the treatment of tropical diseases, the Peace Corps wouldn't let her leave the country until her samples showed up clean. There was no way I was leaving Panama without Ronnie. So for three more days, I shat in a cup and carried my paper bag to the lab with her name on it. The lab reported to the Peace Corps: There must have been a mistake in the first batch or a miracle! Parasites gone! Ronnie could go home.

In the early winter of 1970, when I was 23, I moved to Washington, DC, and was hired as a bookkeeper/office manager at *Hard Times*. This was a weekly newsletter published and written mostly by James Ridgeway and Andrew Kopkind. They were true muckraking journalists—smart, radical, really good writers. I had no skills or interest to qualify me as a bookkeeper/office manager, but they told me I could try writing in my spare time. I really wanted to be in DC because I wanted to be involved in radical politics, and what better place to do that but in the belly of the beast. I wrote well enough, so I took the job. I asked my mother to teach me the basics of bookkeeping, which she did, and I figured out how to collect and sort the mail, order supplies, and answer the phone. Pretty soon they were giving me assignments; I was researching stories, covering events, and writing about them. I was pretty good, and they helped me get better.

We got a tip that the National Welfare Rights Organization (NWRO) was going to have an action at the Department of Health, Education, and Welfare (HEW) (this later became Health and Human Services). I rode my motor scooter from *Hard Times'* one-room office in Georgetown to the block-long HEW building, parked, and found the NWRO delegation forming on the sidewalk. There were about fifty women, almost all African American, led by activist and organizer Johnnie Tillmon. The NWRO had been trying for months to get a meeting with Robert Finch, who was Richard Nixon's HEW Secretary, but Finch wouldn't see them and wouldn't even listen to their requests—which over time, because of Finch's refusal to see them, became demands—for a more generous and comprehensive safety net for poor people, especially women and children. So Johnnie was going to lead the group to Finch's office and make the meeting happen.

In those pre-9/11 days, it was possible to walk into a government building, get on an elevator, ride to the top, get off and walk to the office of an official as highly placed as the secretary of a department without going through a heavy-duty security system. Getting inside the office was another matter. Johnnie and her troops led the way up, and, by the time the growing cadre of reporters and camera people got there, the NWRO women had breached the inner office. Given advance notice they were coming, Finch had already made his escape.

After the breach, armed security men had arrayed themselves just outside the office and were warning the reporters, "Do not enter this office. You are trespassing on government property if you enter this office."

Sitting behind Finch's large desk, looking completely pleased with herself, Johnnie was engaging in a call-and-response with the guards. Every time they yelled at us to stay out, she yelled back, "Come on in. This is now the office of the NWRO, and you're welcome here."

I was at the front of the media pack and couldn't think of one reason why I shouldn't go in. I certainly didn't think anybody was going to shoot me, and I loved the boldness of these women and the power they were radiating. So I walked across the threshold, and then the rest of the media followed. Johnnie spoke for about ten minutes before more security guards came and told the women to leave or face arrest. They left. I raced back to the office and wrote up the story.

~

In the four months between my return from Panama and my arrival in DC, I had read an article called "The Myth of the Vaginal Orgasm" by Anne Koedt. This important essay debunked the notion that women who did not have vaginal orgasms were frigid, and placed the clitoris at the center of women's sexual pleasure. Just the concept that women could and should decide what made us feel good was revolutionary at this time. It was the first time I had read or heard anything about what was being called Women's Liberation, and I thought that focusing on orgasms was relevant only to a bourgeois movement for white, middle-class women. I was really hoping that Women's Liberation would mean that I wouldn't have to be sexual with men anymore, and I was still trying desperately not to think about being sexual with women. So I really did not want to talk about any kind of orgasm. More than that, I didn't yet understand how fundamental to everyone's liberation is the right to control our own bodies.

Nevertheless, I put on a brave face and went to my first Women's Liberation meeting in January 1970, and, much to my delight, nobody even mentioned their orgasms. Instead, we spent the night arguing about which came first, patriarchy or capitalism. I was so happy to be in a room full of women all talking politics and political theory, but I held back. I was still operating out of my head. My heart wasn't there yet, but it was beginning to move. As I continued to attend and then participated in Women's Liberation meetings, I began to understand that this "Women's Liberation" thing might mean that I wouldn't have to pretend to be attracted to men or not be attracted to women. This was incredibly exciting, and I wondered if I might actually find a real home in this movement. Although I hadn't had a woman lover yet, I was opening the door to the closet I was in.

It was around this time that I met Sharon Deevy. Sharon had short, dark hair and a spray of freckles across her nose. In every picture I have of her, she is wearing a vest and a newsboy cap. She smiled a lot, and her voice was surprisingly deep for someone as small as she was. Sharon was very good friends with Joan Biren. I knew Joan from Mount Holyoke. She was a year ahead of me and was already a legend in certain circles for her intelligence and her political acumen. Unbeknownst to me (oh, if only I had known that there was someone like me who was a lesbian), she was having a sexual relationship with a woman. At Mount Holyoke, Joan and I both majored in political science. We were both active in student government. We were both politically on the left. We looked enough alike that people often mistook us for each other. Short, dark hair—mine curly, hers wavy—Jewish, East Coast.

Joan, Sharon, and I went to a huge demonstration together in support of the Chicago Seven in front of the Watergate building, and we were arrested. The Chicago Seven were originally the Chicago Eight, until Black Panther cofounder Bobby Seale was separated from them. These radical men, including Tom Hayden, Abbie Hoffman, and Jerry Rubin, had been arrested following the disruption of the 1968 Democratic Convention in Chicago. The trial was a sham, the accused were being railroaded, and everyone, including the notorious Judge Julius Hoffman—who had ordered that Bobby Seale be bound and gagged—was performing acts of political theater. We were demonstrating at the Watergate because that's where Nixon's attorney general, John Mitchell, lived. (The Watergate building would become the scene of Nixon's undoing, but that was later.)

Without intending to, we found ourselves at the front of the large and very loud crowd, and we didn't hear the police order to disperse. When the cops charged, we ended up trapped between their lines. It was my first arrest. My few hours in a DC jail cell provided me with another example—not unlike the NWRO action—of what I thought of as the real meaning of sisterhood, a kind of solidarity, support, and taking care of each other that was inspirational.

Before the summer of 1970, Jim and Andy told me they didn't have enough money to keep me on the *Hard Times* payroll for the summer (my salary was $75 a week) but they offered to buy me a See America First bus ticket so I could travel around the country and write stories. I jumped at the chance. I started at a big anti-war conference in Madison and alternately hitched or took the Greyhound all the way to California. I wanted to write a story about the Women's Liberation Movement, so I got contacts from the feminist newspaper *off our backs* subscription list. I would just call up women and ask them if I could stay with them and write about what was happening in the movement where they lived. They almost always said yes. For two months, I talked to women in cities like Denver and San Francisco and little towns like Halstead, Kansas. Even in Halstead, population less than two thousand, there was a Women's Liberation group. We were starting to be everywhere.

The Chicano movement was also rising up, and Jim and Andy asked me to research and write a story on their movement to reclaim the land they said had been stolen from them. When I came back to DC at the end of the summer of 1970, I had no trouble writing a strong story about the Chicano struggle, and it was published soon after. But I couldn't write the Women's Liberation story. Suddenly, it felt too personal. I didn't want to share what I had learned—about the movement and about myself—with my male editors and mostly male readership. Meeting all these feminist women, hearing their stories, experiencing the communities they were building had opened up something in me. This was real. Unlike discussions I'd had in the past, this was not an argument about capitalism versus patriarchy. This was change, and I was falling in love with it.

Jim and Andy were in the process of selling *Hard Times* to the radical magazine *Ramparts*, and, although I would soon be out of a job, I was not upset. I found myself being pulled at by something else. I was ready to give my full attention to women.

∾

Sharon and Joan invited me to have lunch with them, and I was happy to do it. They had something they wanted to tell me—they were lesbians, and they were lovers. I could tell they were not sure how I would react, but they needn't have worried. I thought my head would explode with joy. Here were two "normal" women—not monsters at all. Smart, funny, good-looking, kind. And lesbians!

Sharon and Joan were the first out lesbians I knew, and their coming out to me was a revelation. It wasn't just theoretical, and it wasn't just me. I thought they were incredibly brave, and if they could be brave, so could I. Without any hesitation I told them that I too was a lesbian.

～

In the fall of 1970, I moved into a newly formed women's commune on 18th Street in the Adams Morgan section of Northwest Washington. Among the five original residents were Tasha Petersen and Susan Hathaway, just in from their solidarity work with the Chicago Eight in Chicago. Only one of us had a job, but we shared everything we had, ate a lot of rice and beans, and got by without difficulty. We spent our days going to meetings of Women Against Imperialism, Women Against Racism, Women Against Population Control, etc. We spent our nights getting stoned, eating donuts, and riding around town spray-painting anti-war slogans on DC's signs and government buildings. We were dismissive and disdainful of the male-dominated anti-war movement, but even as our understanding of woman-oppression and women's liberation grew, we found ourselves at least somewhat in alignment with the Black Panther Party, which had an active chapter in DC. It wasn't just the defiance and militancy that appealed to me. It was the service. The Panthers were feeding people, providing healthcare, schools. They had the idea that people could be transformed politically through having the experience of someone taking care of their needs. This was a revolutionary concept: the idea that *protesting* injustice is necessary but not sufficient; that building a powerful movement also required that we *demonstrate* what a just society would look like. The Panthers planted a seed in me that would later blossom.

Meanwhile, Sharon and I became lovers. I wasn't sexually attracted to Sharon, but I liked her and we were all taking the position that sexual attraction was just another capitalistic patriarchal lie designed to keep women tied to men in nuclear families. Everything we had been taught by our parents, schools, religions, TV, and government was that sex was sacred and special and meant love and marriage. Naturally, we rejected that and held the belief that your friends should be your lovers. And so Sharon was my first woman lover, even though she and Joan were still lovers, because in addition to smashing the state we were also smashing monogamy. I understood that Sharon's relationship with Joan was primary, and that was fine with me. I had been fantasizing about making love with a woman for so long that I knew exactly what to do, but I didn't have my first real lesbian thrill until I met Jennifer Woodul in the outfield at a women's softball game. Jennifer and I fell in love, and I lost interest in smashing monogamy.

Washington, DC, was alive with radical political activity, and a lot of that was centered on the Women's Liberation Movement and the growing visibility of lesbians in the Movement. Women were pouring in from all over the country, and our 18th Street house, as the first self-identified women's house in Washington, was a hub for women from all over the country who were traveling to DC to participate in one political rally/activity/protest or another. Our door was always open to women.

Rita Mae Brown moved down from New York, where she had been involved in Radicalesbians and was one of the authors of "Woman-Identified Woman," a manifesto that made the case for the primacy of Lesbianism to the Women's Movement. Rita Mae was already known as a writer and speaker, and for her unsuccessful (at that time) attempt to force NOW to address lesbian issues.

Helaine Harris was nineteen years old when she arrived from Albuquerque. Nancy Myron moved down from New York with a group of lesbians. Lee Schwing was all of eighteen and came to DC as part of Goddard College's internship program for first-year students. Her internship at *off our backs* was supposed to last a couple of months, but she got sidetracked by the Women's Movement and stayed in DC for years.

Coletta Reid was already living a few doors down from the 18th Street women's house with her husband and two children. She was involved with putting out *off our backs*. Charlotte Bunch was active in DC Women's Liberation, and, even in those early days, was a feminist theorist. She was also living with her husband.

Rita organized a consciousness-raising group for all the straight women, which included Susan, Tasha, Coletta, Helaine, Lee, Charlotte, and several other women. It didn't take long for these women to make the logical leap from radical feminism to lesbianism, first in theory and then in practice. The married women left their husbands and soon became lovers with other women. The women who didn't want to come out dropped out, and soon Rita was inviting other lesbians to join the group. Nancy, Joan, Sharon, Jennifer, and I did.

At first, we called ourselves Those Women, because that's what straight Women's Liberationists were calling us. But that didn't last long—we were not about to let anyone define us but ourselves. At Rita's suggestion, all of us except Joan and Sharon moved out of hippie and lefty Northwest DC into gay Capitol Hill. Rita was already renting a house on 12th Street. Jennifer and I moved in with her, and we found two other houses within a few blocks of each other, on 11th and 8th Streets, for everyone else.

We decided to call ourselves The Furies. I was really home.

2 WOMAN-LOVING WOMEN

The Furies—Lesbian and Loud

TWELVE LESBIAN FEMINISTS BECAME THE FURIES. We were all white, rural and urban, working, middle and upper-middle class. We ranged in age from eighteen to twenty-eight. We were furious. We were vibrating with the knowledge that everything we thought was wrong with us was not, and we knew who was responsible and why this was so. We understood the many ways that men believed women's bodies were supposed to belong to them and the many ways that men enforced their ownership. Some raped their wives ("marital rape" had not yet been named and criminalized in the early '70s); some raped their dates (unspoken of publicly as "date rape" until the mid '70s); some raped strangers with impunity; when they went to war, some raped the women and children of their enemies. Some broke and bound women's feet to make them appear more dainty—with the added advantage that women wouldn't be able to run away. Some mutilated women's genitals to control women's "insatiable" sexuality, to ensure virginity before marriage and fidelity after, and to increase male sexual pleasure and deny female pleasure. They did everything they could to control women's reproductive choices (and many still do).

We had all grown up with at least some part of us believing what we were taught about the proper place for girls and women, the proper activities we could engage in, the proper people to love, the proper amount of space to take up, and the proper goals to shoot for so that we could live proper lives.

Now we were alive with the possibilities of turning our self-hatred and self-doubt—about being lesbian, female, poor, too smart, uneducated, not fragile enough, not thin enough, not "pretty" enough—into a powerful movement that declared, in a most loud and unfeminine way, that we loved who we were, that we were beautiful and strong and smart and wise, and that we wanted every woman to come move and change with us. Acting with great seriousness of purpose, we took our rage and our joy and channeled them into developing a political theory of lesbian feminism, and for nine months we tried to live the theory.

This was the core of our ideological thought:

- Sexism is the root of all other oppressions. Lesbian and woman oppression will not end by smashing capitalism, racism, imperialism, and all the other forms of domination. Sexism is not the bad behavior of some men; it is a system of oppression that operates on a personal level as well as on an institutional and structural level.

- Lesbianism is the essential revolutionary component in upending the system. We opt out of being in relationship to men and therefore we challenge male supremacy in a fundamental way. We do not need men for anything. And we will not allow ourselves to be divided by men.

- Because lesbians are outcasts from every culture, we will be natural allies across class, race, and national lines. Lesbians have the most to gain by actively engaging in ending class, race, and national supremacy.

Lesbian feminism *necessarily* includes struggles against racism and classism; overthrowing the patriarchy, ending male supremacy, *inherently* means ending race, class, and national supremacy. Women of color, for example, will not be liberated by feminism if we do not end racism. Vietnamese women (who were being victimized by the US war machine) will not be liberated by feminism if we do not end US imperialism. (We understood intersectionality before there was a term for it.)

- We believed that the personal is political, that how people act in their personal relationships is not just individual, but is often a function of social structures and systems, and is an important measure of one's politics. You can't give speeches about the importance of nonviolence and then go home and beat your wife. We also believed that the political is personal, that sexual attraction and orientation are socially constructed rather than biologically determined.

- Therefore, lesbianism is a political choice. Because they involve power and dominance, relationships between women and men are essentially political. It is therefore critically important for women to withdraw their energies and their presence from these inherently unequal relationships. Additionally, to see lesbianism as merely a matter of sexuality is to define women in male terms—as sexual beings and nothing more.

- We chose to operate collectively and to live communally. We rejected authority and imposed hierarchies. We did not reject leadership. In fact, we considered ourselves leaders of the lesbian feminist movement.

These ideas did not emerge full-blown from our very fertile minds. We studied and reported to each other on how other revolutions had come to power and then become totalitarian. I was in the group that read Isaac Deutscher's *Stalin: A Political Biography*. The others studied the Chinese revolution or the rise of the Nazi party. We read Friedrich Engels's *The Origin of the Family, Private Property and the State*. We looked at other progressive political movements—from the women's suffrage movement to the Black Panther Party—to try to understand where they had succeeded and why they had failed. There was a flourishing underground press that produced hundreds of newspapers and pamphlets, and, when we could get our hands on them, we read them. We were most interested in those that came from Women's Liberation (*off our backs, Ain't I a Woman, Big Mama Rag* to name a few) and from the Black Power movement (*The Black Panther*). We read *The Ladder*, a lesbian magazine published by the Daughters of Bilitis, the first nationally distributed lesbian publication. We read books on the women's suffrage movement, and we looked for information about strong women whose stories we may have known, but whose strength, and perhaps their lesbianism, had been hidden. Robin Morgan's *Sisterhood Is Powerful* came out in 1970, and we gobbled that up too. We also found time to read the few lesbian novels that we could find, like *The Well of Loneliness* (Radclyffe Hall), and occasionally we found one where the lesbian protagonist didn't die in the end.

We gathered what we could from all of these sources, but none of them addressed the totality of who we were becoming. We felt an urgent need for a coherent theory of lesbian feminism that examined all systems of power and oppression through a woman-identified lens, and that offered a vision—with ourselves as models—of a revolutionary future.

Within a few months of our move to Capitol Hill, we thought we had enough clarity to start spreading the word and seeing who would join us. In the fall of 1971, we decided to produce a monthly newspaper, *The Furies* (which rarely came out on a monthly schedule and, in any case, had no news). We wanted to spread our ideas among lesbians and convince straight feminists to leave heterosexuality behind and become lesbians. We saw ourselves as a vanguard cell readying ourselves to lead a mass movement of women. Eventually, we thought we would form coalitions with other sufficiently developed cells and movements to end all oppression. But that was a long way off.

A lot of our political development now centered around *The Furies*—which issues did we think most urgently needed addressing and what would our approach be? The first issue came out in January 1972. The contents of that issue were pretty typical of what would follow:

- "The Furies" (lead article introducing ourselves and our politics) by me.
- "Such a Nice Girl" (understanding heterosexual and class privilege) by Sharon Deevey.
- "Women: Weak or Strong" (a regular column on physical conditioning) by Lee Schwing.
- "The Dentist" (a short story) by me.
- "Roxanne Dunbar: How a Female Heterosexual Serves the Interest of Male Supremacy" (a critique of an article Roxanne wrote for another journal that lumped the Lesbian Feminist movement in with the male New Left) by Rita Mae Brown.
- Poems including "A History of Lesbianism" and "Detroit Annie, Hitchhiking" by Judy Grahn

- "Lesbians in Revolt: Male Supremacy Quakes and Quivers" (a further explication of our politics) by Charlotte Bunch
- "Queen Christina: Lesbian Ruler of Sweden" (a brief bio) by Helaine Harris
- "Gossip" (how gossip is used to hurt political women) by Rita Mae Brown
- "The Price is Wrong" (explanation of basic capitalist economics) by Susan Hathaway
- "What's Going On?" (reports and announcements from lesbian groups around the country).
- Photos by JEB (Joan Biren) and others
- Drawings by Nancy Myron and others

Once we started publishing, we started getting response. Much of it was encouraging and gratifying. There were lesbians—and some straight women—who were inspired by our politics and excited by our boldness. Women met in study groups to read it and discuss the articles. An Oakland, California, group of lesbians and straight women called Women for Armed Struggle studied revolutionary movements, and they were thrilled to finally find one with a feminist consciousness and analysis.

Some of the response was critical. There were women and other newly formed lesbian feminist groups in the country who were also thinking big thoughts, and they did not always agree with us on every point. Minneapolis-based Radical Feminists 28 engaged in a dialogue with us via letters. They thought that instead of asking ourselves—which they said we continually did—"What is the revolutionary thing to do?" that we should be asking ourselves "What is the necessary thing to do for the revolution?" Our question implied a commitment to process, to living out now, as much as possible, the principles that we were fighting for. The end we get to is determined, at least in part, by the means we use to get there. But their question implied a concession to the ends—we believed that "by whatever means necessary" would not bring us to the true revolution, the end of patriarchy, but would only result in a change of who held power. We spent many hours in meetings analyzing the critics' points of view and crafting responses. I don't ever remember us changing our minds, changing our positions, about anything, even one time. We were just completely sure that we were right.

We pushed ourselves to imagine the future, to figure out what we wanted a new world to look like. How would the economy be organized? What kind of government would we have? Would there be a military? This in and of itself was a huge change. We stopped participating in Women Against Imperialism, Women Against Racism, Women Against (fill in the blank) and began defining our political work in terms of what we were *for*. I was beginning to understand the power of a positive vision.

Communal living, implemented through a lens of class consciousness and class analysis, was one part of our vision that we engaged in from the start. We developed an income-sharing system that reflected our class differences. The women with the most privilege contributed the most to the common pot, and the women with the least privilege put in less. Women with more education and marketable skills were expected to earn more and contribute more so that women with less education and skills would not have to work longer hours to earn enough to live. After much experimenting, we settled on a percentage system, with some contributing as little as 20% of their earnings or an $80 minimum to some contributing 50% or more. We actually didn't have a rigid formula—we worked out in discussion how much each of us would contribute. We made a collective decision to send one working-class woman, who had supported herself since high school, to printing school so that she would have a marketable skill, and one that we expected would be useful for us down the line. We divided up the cars that individual women owned so that every one of our three communal houses had at least one car.

~

Did we have it all figured out and were we living the lives of true lesbian feminist revolutionaries? Not exactly.

We were somewhat successful at working collectively, but there were clear and unacknowledged power imbalances in our group. Rita Mae Brown had been the driving force in bringing the group together, and she held a position in the center of The Furies as long as the collective existed. Rita stood around 5′ 4″ tall with a lean body that seemed fit and full of a kind of wired energy. Her hair was dark brown and short (everyone had short hair—we believed that women kept their hair long to please men). Her thick, dark eyebrows drew attention to her brown eyes that could seduce—or shoot daggers. Her smile was warm and welcoming. She always dressed in a style more like a gay man than a '70s dyke—fitted jackets and ankle boots—no patched jeans and flannel shirts for her.

It hadn't taken me long to know that I wanted to work with her. She was smart, a dazzling strategist, charming and charismatic. She exuded a kind of power that drew me to her. She was at ease with her sexuality and her butchness. She could be a loving and patient teacher—which she was for me—and a ferocious fighter whose words could slash to pieces anyone who opposed her. Rita came from a working-class background and had the most developed class analysis among us, and all this, combined with her natural magnetism, helped to solidify her dominant position in the collective. Until eventually it didn't. We never discussed the power dynamics inside The Furies as a group.

Within a few months of her move to DC, Rita had brought Charlotte Bunch out of the closet. Charlotte was a brilliant political theorist and was highly regarded by the greater Women's Liberation Movement. In addition to her knowledge of the Women's Suffrage Movement, she had a well-developed sense of globalism, understanding early on that women's rights were human rights. I had immense respect for both of them, and when I got back a piece I had written for the newspaper with their edits and suggestions, I took them to heart. When Rita and Charlotte were in agreement, it was difficult to argue with them, and who would want to, anyway? But when they were not, Charlotte would often accede to Rita, and I found myself usually agreeing with Rita. Their relationship lasted a very short time, and then Rita and Tasha became lovers.

We politicized all our disagreements with each other, even the smallest things. For instance, Rita, Jennifer, and I lived together in the 12th Street house, and when we had meetings of the whole collective at our house, we always hid the cookies. We did this because whenever Lee came over, she would head into our kitchen and eat all the cookies. Lee was entitled, we thought. Lee had privilege. We couldn't just say that we didn't want to share our cookies with Lee, our comrade. That would have reflected badly on us. Somehow it was easier to share our cars than our cookies. Lee was the Goddard intern who came to DC for a semester and got seduced, first by the Women's Liberation movement, and then by Lesbian Feminism. She was teaching us Tae Kwon Do and generally led whatever efforts we engaged in towards physical fitness. I recently spoke to Lee and reminded her about how she made a beeline for our cookies, and she laughed. "I was always hungry," she said. She was eighteen and still a growing girl, but Rita, Jennifer, and I turned it into a class issue.

There was another disagreement we had that was very complicated and much more serious, and some of The Furies are still dealing with the consequences.

Two of The Furies had daughters living with us, aged six and two, and two others had "adopted" a two-month-old infant girl (her birth mother had passed through the 18th Street house and left her with the two women). A few months after we became a collective, Rita raised the question of whether we could be an effective revolutionary cell if we had children, and we spent quite a few meetings discussing this. The children did take up a lot of time and energy. They were children—they needed to be fed and bathed and read to and played with and put to sleep. They got sick and had to be taken to the doctor. They outgrew their shoes and their clothes and needed new ones. They needed attention.

Not surprisingly, our collective did not place a high value on mothering. Motherhood was supposed to be the pinnacle of a woman's life, the ultimate fulfillment of female purpose on the planet. Of course, we rejected this notion. We considered this another male myth designed to keep women stuck in their homes, isolated from each other, with little to stimulate their intellects, economically dependent—and so, tied to men. My own mother worked as a bookkeeper all the time I was growing up, and she also had primary responsibility for keeping our house in order, shopping and cooking for the family, and raising three daughters. Her job was not challenging or stimulating, and I doubt she could have supported herself—to say nothing of the three of us—on her salary, nor would I say that she found much joy in raising her children. A better description of her state of mind might be frustrated, tired, irritable, and dissatisfied. But even if my mother, or any of our mothers, had managed to "have it all," the "all" they had was not the "all" that we wanted.

We were not looking to have careers. We were looking to make a revolution. We were warriors, and we were taking on the whole world—government, church, corporate structure, media, and the male Left. There were times we fantasized about a blissful post-revolutionary world, but just as often we saw ourselves on the run, underground, taking up arms—who knew what? Would we even be alive in ten years? In five? It was dangerous to be a radical political leader or visionary in the US. People were being assassinated (Martin Luther King, Jr., Malcolm X, Robert Kennedy, Fred Hampton) and others were being thrown in prison (Ericka Huggins, Angela Davis, and much of the Black Panther Party. The only reason we still roamed free was that the government didn't take lesbians seriously. But we knew that our politics posed the ultimate threat to the whole patriarchal capitalist system and that, once our movement was large enough, we would lose our cloak of invisibility. (Later this proved to be the case when the FBI attempted to infiltrate many lesbian and feminist collectives.)

This was not an atmosphere in which to raise children. To the extent that the mothers, or anyone else, spoke of their emotional ties to the children, they were quickly reminded that we based our political decisions on what we insisted was clear-eyed analysis, not emotions, that such behavior was completely inimical to who we were.

In Volume 1, Issue 2 of *The Furies*, Sharon and Coletta wrote an article called "Emotionalism—Downward Spiral," and it hinted at emerging splits in The Furies.

> Middle-class women have encouraged a cult of "getting in touch with your feelings," and basing political decisions on how you feel. A lot of that over-emphasis is in reaction to the emotional sterility of middle-class life. But much also comes from the way in which

middle-class women use their feelings to manipulate others. This happened in our group. The constant verbalizing and psychologizing of the middle-class women about their relationships was especially oppressive to the working-class lesbians in the group and was directed toward control of them and others in those relationships.

The explicit arguments for keeping the children focused on the cruelty to the girls and their mothers of sending them off, and the belief that we could raise the next generation of revolutionary women and keep them free from the internalized homophobia and sexism that had tormented us growing up.

But the impetus to send the children away was neither entirely focused on the needs of the children, nor entirely on the needs of the revolution. There were other motives that were spoken about in private, but never to the whole group. Rita Mae, for example, often expressed resentment to Tasha, her lover at the moment, about the amount of time Tasha was spending with her daughter rather that with Rita. And there was growing tension between Rita and Joan over control. For the most part, the issues between them were insignificant; the struggle seemed to be over Rita's leadership role in the collective and Joan's resistance to it. I put myself on Rita's side most of the time, and I found Joan's wrestling for control with Rita highly irritating.

But the question of what to do about the children was not an insignificant disagreement. Joan and Sharon had "adopted" the infant, and argued strongly against sending the children away. Ultimately, everyone, including the other mothers, agreed that the children had to go. Joan and Sharon, after many meetings and much resistance, finally consented. The three children were not sent off into the wilderness and within a few years two were back with their mothers. Each of them went to good homes with loving adults.

But the issue of the children gave us—with Rita leading the way and me right behind her—the pretext for getting Joan and Sharon out of the collective. We no longer wanted to live with the tensions that came from the leadership struggle.

The decision to send the children away was perhaps The Furies' lowest moment. Though it may have made perfect sense as a choice for revolutionaries, it was heartless. In our attempts to not be ruled by our emotions, we too often allowed ourselves no space to express them, and maybe even to feel them.

I was not sad to see the children go. I believed that we had work to do that was much more serious than raising children, and I fully supported Rita. For the nine months or so that it lasted, I was delighted to have her light shine on me. I had never before been part of the "in" crowd, and I liked it. To be so close to power, even in the small world of The Furies, was a new and heady experience for me, and my closeness to Rita conferred power on me as well.

As time went on, however, I began to see things about her that troubled me. I don't know if having consolidated her position inside The Furies emboldened her, or if she was just starting to feel confined by the requirements of collective living, working, and thinking. But she was making decisions and launching projects on her own. I noticed her saying things about other collective members that I knew were not true.

As I started to watch Rita with a critical eye, I began to understand how even the most ardent, revolutionary, smart, politically developed lesbian feminist could exercise personal power in ways that were indirect, manipulative, devious, and ultimately harmful. What we would have called "male." I felt betrayed by her. I thought we were comrades, and that we would be forever. I brought the full weight of my judgment onto her without remembering that we had no role models for feminist leadership; we had no experience of true power sharing; we had no skill at balancing our individual wants and needs with the collective. Jennifer and I would lie in bed at night and whisper about what we thought was going on and who else we might talk to about what we were thinking.

But these cracks in the collective were well-hidden from the rest of the world, and we continued to exercise a kind of power with lesbians and feminists because of our analysis and vision. Women all over the country anxiously waited for their copy of *The Furies* to arrive every month or so. We were not the only women or lesbians thinking both ideologically and strategically, but, because we had the newspaper, we seemed to have the greatest reach. We inspired people and we infuriated them—which was also a kind of power. I loved meeting women who were learning from what we were writing, who were thinking about what we were saying, and who were making changes because of it. I believed that at some point all these diverse groups and individual women would come together under the leadership of The Furies.

One measure of The Furies' impact came in 2015 when the house on 11th Street, the house where we physically produced *The Furies*, was listed in the National Register of Historic Places. The nomination described the collective and the newspaper as

> a national center of lesbian feminist separatism....Though the actual programmatic accomplishments of the collective may seem scant, their ideological and intellectual role in defining the terms of debate as lesbianism and feminism defined themselves and confronted issues of sexism, male supremacy, economic difference and oppression, racism, and gender identity was huge.

I loved the time we spent in the collective and working on the newspaper, hashing out our politics. We sat in meetings and pushed each other. I learned how to think big and small at the same time—with vision and with strategy. Every article that any of us wrote went through a rigorous editing process, and I became a better writer because of it. Rita in particular helped me write with more clarity and more rhythm, but everyone made suggestions about content and style.

At the same time, Rita was acting more individualistically, and we began to question her commitment. We finally confronted Rita as a group, but she made it clear that she was not going to change, and we realized she had to go. I think that she was ready to strike out on her own in any case. She had started writing *Rubyfruit Jungle*, and the collective was becoming too demanding for her.

Within a month, we dissolved the collective. Rita really had been the core, and, without her, there wasn't enough to hold us together. The rest of us left without rancor and found numerous ways to stay connected over time. Some of us continued publishing the newspaper, and, eventually, new women were brought in to work on *The Furies*. The Furies collective lasted less than a year and published the first seven issues, the first in January 1972 and the last in fall 1972. This is astonishing given how much we did, how much we learned, and the impact we had. It feels like time moved much more slowly then. Three more issues were published after the collective dissolved, with the final issue appearing in May–June 1973.

Rita once said that the true test of our success was the collective members themselves. She was certainly not the only one of us who was ready to strike out in a new direction. Coletta left to co-found Diana Press, one of the first independent feminist publishers, and Nancy later worked there and made important contributions. Charlotte and Rita helped found

Quest: A Feminist Quarterly. Lee and Helaine were among the founders of Women in Distribution, one of the first feminist distribution companies. Joan became a great documentarian of lesbian lives through her photography. Jennifer and I went on to found Olivia Records.

I was a different person at the end of The Furies than I was at the beginning. Working collectively suited me. It let me flower as an individual while providing a structured, supportive community. I had a political vision that I had helped develop, and this helped me understand my place in the world and the path I wanted to follow. I had a deep understanding of class that I would try to apply in every aspect of my life, and that helped inform the choices I made in the future. I fully embraced myself as a lesbian and had hot and joyous sex that was better than anything I had ever imagined. If I wasn't going to be able to play professional baseball, making a lesbian feminist revolution was not a bad alternative.

3 FREEST FANCY

Meg, Music, Magic

A COUPLE OF MONTHS BEFORE we went our separate ways, The Furies collective decided that we needed more allies inside the DC lesbian community. We were young, angry, separatist, liberated, sure of ourselves, arrogant. And alone. It was early winter of 1972 and we worried that our self-imposed isolation would be dangerous for us if the US government came after us. We wanted friends we could turn to, who would stand with us or at least for us, who might be willing to hide us if it came to that. We were given assignments of people to organize—to bring to our side. My assignment was Meg Christian.

Meg was "old gay," meaning she had come out before the advent of the Women's Liberation Movement. She was trained as a classical guitarist and made her living giving guitar lessons and performing pop and folk music at the local clubs—including Mr. Henry's and Clyde's. She had a sweet voice and accompanied herself with her nylon-string guitar. She did covers of material by Joni Mitchell, Carole King, Dusty Springfield, Cris Williamson, and others. She changed the pronouns from "he" to "you." She took pop songs and sang them straight but with a wink to the knowing, songs like The Four Seasons' "Sherry" ("Sherry, can you come out tonight?"). She sang with her eyes closed. We would go see her perform occasionally, and while we liked the music and the seeming slyness with which she sang to the women in the room and ignored the men, we didn't think of her as political. She was mostly singing love songs. Really, not very revolutionary. But a couple of times I would go into the ladies' room and find a woman in tears. Why? Because she felt like Meg was paying attention to her, was singing to her, and not to her date, and it literally moved her to tears.

Meg and I knew each other, of course, both of us part of the larger lesbian community in DC. I decided to make my move at the Phase One—one of the two mafia-run lesbian bars, and the one The Furies usually hung out at. In my naivete and arrogance, I thought she would be thrilled to dance with a Fury. My plan was to ask her to dance a slow number and then, while we were swaying to the music, convince her to be more political and to be willing to rush to our defense in case of attack.

I sat with three of my Furies friends around a round wooden table in the bar. The table, like the floor, was sticky with old beer. The light was so dim we could barely see each other. Only Alan, the bearded manager who poured drinks and kept an eye on everyone from behind the bar was in the light. We were all slugging beers from the bottle, talking loudly and gruffly, trying to work up our courage to ask our assignments to dance. In anticipation of my big move on Meg, I had worn my good jeans—the ones without the holes in the knees—and a flannel shirt tucked in. I thought I looked pretty spiffy.

Gladys Knight's voice came booming out of the juke box—"Midnight Train to Georgia." My time had come. I sidled over to where Meg was sitting at the bar with a glass of pink rosé. She was talking to a mutual friend, and the moment there was a pause in the conversation, I tapped her on the shoulder and asked her if she wanted to dance. "Sure," she said and slid off the bar stool. We put our arms around each other in the "feminist" way of dancing—no roles for us. Meg was about five inches shorter than me, her hair was soft and feathery, and she was wearing a see-through blouse and brown polyester pants—all of which told me that I should lead. Actually, our dancing consisted of moving our feet in no discernible pattern and not going very far—the dance floor was only 100 square feet and it was crowded. The only way she could hear anything I had to say would be if I whispered in her ear, which I did and told her she was a good dancer. Then she moved her left hand down my back and planted it right above where my butt began. It was electric. I was totally turned on. How could this be? I was lovers with Jennifer Woodul—and I loved her. And she loved me. And it was the first mutually loving relationship I had ever had. So how could I be turned on by Meg?

I'm not sure if Meg and I ever talked about my ideas for how she could be a better lesbian and supporter of The Furies. I am sure that I started being slightly obsessed with her. Jennifer and I had previously agreed that it would be okay if one of us wanted to sleep with someone else, so I wasn't worried about being unfaithful to Jennifer. Meg and I went on a date, to see Lily Tomlin at the Cellar Door. We sat in the balcony and held hands. It might have been that night or it might have been another soon after when we went to her apartment. I asked her to sing for me and to keep her eyes open and look at me. She sang a Judy Mayhan song, "Freest Fancy." She looked at me and sang "I hold you very dear/You've made it very clear/You are my freest fancy/My craziest dream." I was a puddle. We made love. Again and again.

I insisted that her cats, Elf and Sappho (probably half of all the cats who lived with lesbians in the '70s were named Sappho), be barred from the bedroom. She complied but she was not happy about it, and I thought this would never work because I did not like cats and I wasn't about to compromise. The second time I went to her apartment, I brought catnip mice for everyone. The bedroom door stayed open. Problem solved. Jennifer and I broke up. Everyone in The Furies was mad at me. How could I leave wonderful Jennifer (who was and is wonderful)—a Fury, a smart and political woman, a member of our revolutionary cadre—for apolitical Meg who sings "you" instead of "he" but won't sing "she," who sings mostly love songs (with her eyes closed), and who does not study revolutionary thinking or feminist theory. I moved out of the 12th Street house, where Jennifer and I had been living with Rita, and moved into the 11th Street house with Nancy Myron and Tasha Peterson. Also living there was Evelyn, a slightly neurotic orange cat who had been passed around (she had originally lived with Elf and Sappho but didn't get along with them). One night Evelyn beat down the door to my bedroom, jumped onto my bed, slid under the covers, put her furry body right next to my belly, started purring, and fell asleep. She clearly knew how to win me over. We stayed together for many years until she died.

There's an old lesbian joke:

"What does a lesbian bring on a second date?"

"A U-Haul."

Meg and I, along with Evelyn, Elf, Sappho, and Sappho's new son Nipper, moved in together. We rented a furnished house in Anacostia. Our neighbors were old retired white heterosexual couples and young black heterosexual couples with children. Nobody really knew what to make of us. The rental agent, a Mr. Zagami, tried many times to get us to tell him what our relationship was to each other. He would tell us about other single women he knew, some of whom were "in the life." We just nodded. As bold and furious as we were, we were also terrified of losing our jobs (I was teaching Spanish to kindergarteners and first graders at a private school in DC), losing the house, getting beat up, and having other bad things happen to us if people found out we were lesbian lovers. Our cats all lived outside and in, and when they were out and I wanted to call them in for dinner, I would not call "Sappho." I called her "Flaffo" or "Baffo." I was sure if the neighbors knew we had a cat named Sappho they would know who we were. But we began to make a life together, and we even invented our own language.

Meg had been fired from a couple of club gigs for bringing in the "wrong clientele," meaning lesbians, so we rarely came to a show in a group of more than two or three. But more and more small groups of lesbians started coming to see her, and she was having a hard time keeping jobs. This infuriated me. This was a prime example of lesbian oppression.

Within a month of our having become lovers, in April 1972, I decided to write Meg a letter, which may seem strange since we were living together. But I had a lot to say and I wanted to be clear and I didn't want to end up yelling at her which I thought I was likely to do if I just told her what I thought.

> I'm not an artist and I don't pretend to know anything about the drive to create beautiful music that keeps you going. But I am a revolutionary and I know about the drive to create a beautiful world that keeps me going, so maybe its [sic] not so different, or maybe it is. I don't know. I guess one of the big differences is what we both do to get out of feeling like shit and to stop being oppressed, and I think that what you do keeps you oppressed and keeps you from being in control of your life the way you want to be.

I then proceeded to excoriate the men who owned the clubs and sat in the audiences and who had the power to determine if she would continue working there. I berated her for wanting their approval and for twisting herself into knots to get it. And then:

> So then the question is, why do you need them? Who are you singing for? If they are just a means to an end, what is the end? Is it to be able to sing beautiful songs to millions of them, and maybe in the process reach a few women? OK. You want to reach women and you want to do it with music. But isn't there a way to do it without messing yourself up? There are a million lesbians in the country who have never heard you. Do they have to wait 10 years or however long it takes you to fight your way through all the male shit? Do you know what a turn-on it is to hear you do "A Case of You" to a woman? The pigs at the Assembly [a local club] don't and never will. I do. And there's a quicker way to reach all those lesbians and other reachables than through the route you're taking….
>
> Why don't you make music for lesbians? Why don't you make tapes for every lesbian group in the country? I bet you could cut a record and distribute it yourself. If they heard you once, they'd never stop buying. I'm serious.

I ended with a plea.

> Really think about it, OK? Don't get super-defensive. Unless you want to scream at me now, and then you can. Also this is not an ultimatum or anything; all previous commitments, expectations, desires, etc., still stand (for me).

She didn't scream at me, or get super defensive. She was skeptical but willing. She was tired of the club scene, tired of having to hide her true self, tired of getting fired. I told her that I would try to get her bookings at women's centers and women's colleges and that Tom, her current manager/booking agent, could continue to book her in the DC clubs.

She started calling what she did Women's Music and defined it as music that speaks honestly and realistically to women's lives. Women's Music was woman-centered. It was not about men or women's relationships to men. I think this was the first time anyone used that term, but it never seemed like we were creating something new. It seemed a natural outgrowth of the combining of our lesbian feminist politics with Meg's music. We didn't know we were creating a category, or a movement. It was just a way to describe what Meg did so I could get her jobs with like-minded women.

Meg had a reel-to-reel tape recorder and a microphone that she set it up in our living room to record a couple of songs. We got them duplicated and I started writing letters and sending tapes out to colleges on the East Coast. And soon we were getting responses. Yes, these women were ready for Women's Music. They were ready to hear their own growing feminist consciousness reflected back to them, ready to be seen as a full human being rather than part of a male fantasy.

On weekends we loaded Meg's little PA system and her guitar into our yellow Toyota station wagon and hit the road. I learned to set up and run the sound. She had started writing her own songs and added these to her repertoire of covers. Her first composition was "Morning Song," which described our house, our cats, our life. Then came "Song to My Mama," which contained the soon-to-be-famous line "I know you know."

> Mama, Mama, do you understand
> Why I've not bound myself to a man?
> Is something buried in your old widow's mind
> That blesses the choice of our own kind?

Oh Mama, Mama.

Mama, Mama, I know you know
But you couldn't survive
If I told you so.
I understand the bounds that you've set
I'll talk of the car and the cat at the vet
But maybe once a year
When I'm a little tight
I'll feel fresh regrets and write
Some cryptic thank-yous for giving me the
    space to find
Such safely unspecific things
As my strength, my freedom, and my life.

And then, Meg's first "hit"—"Ode to a Gym Teacher" with a chorus that has probably been sung by the million lesbians I referenced in my letter.

She was a big tough woman
The first to come along
That showed me being female meant you still
    could be strong
And though graduation meant that we had to part
She'll always be a player on the ballfield of my heart.

She also added a very tongue-in-cheek "Stand by Your Man." She had a totally charming, funny, warm stage presence. To say that audiences loved her would be like saying that it gets a little windy in a Category 5 hurricane.

It was 1972 and women were starved for public manifestations of their excitement, their energy, their self-discovery, their liberation. They—we—were giving birth to ourselves and we wanted our creations to be reflected and represented in every way possible. So when fifty or two hundred or two thousand women came together to a concert of Women's Music—and at this time nobody even knew what that was—the first thing that happened was that they *saw* each other. And, for the first time, were seeing themselves in large numbers. There was a community! There were others like me! I was not the only one! And on the stage was a very talented woman whose music reflected them in so many ways. And she talked to them. She talked about her own life. She related. And they related. There was magic.

Meg and me on our honeymoon. We thought we were
so cool to be staying at the Gay Manor Motel.

4 HELLO HOORAY

Olivia Begins

LTHOUGH I WAS NOT PARTICULARLY sorry when The Furies collective broke up, I missed the focused activity and the political action. I started talking to women about what to do next. I had a sense that I wanted my next project to be media-related and national in scope—like *The Furies* but with more impact. I was starting to think in terms of creating a feminist institution that could have an economic impact, but I really had no idea what it would be. And I thought I wanted writing to be part of it.

In the early days of The Furies, I had gotten a half-time job teaching Spanish to kindergarteners and first graders at the Barrie School in DC, a private school serving mostly African American families. The pay was decent, most of the kids were happy to learn a language that their parents couldn't understand, and the short hours gave me time to do the work I really wanted to do: taking over more and more of the "management" of Meg's career. She was getting booked at women's colleges up and down the East Coast, and she started performing regularly in the basement of the new DC Women's Liberation Center. There would be anywhere from twenty to fifty women there; everyone would sit on the floor and we would pass the hat and take home a few dollars. Because she was now performing in front of her own community and didn't have to worry about losing her job, she started introducing songs by telling stories. They were either funny or poignant or both. Women in the audiences loved hearing them. This represented a performance style that was so different from the distant, impersonal stance most performers took. She was personally connecting. We began to define this as part of Women's Music as well.

I started talking to people about my interest in starting a new project, and, in January 1973, we had the first meeting at our house on Carpenter Street. The person I most wanted to join with me was Jennifer Woodul. Jennifer and I had been lovers for only nine months before Meg and I got together, but Jennifer was very important to me. She was the first woman I loved who loved me. She was smart and funny. She was not afraid to call people on their bullshit and frequently did. In fact, she seemed to be afraid of very little. Jennifer was from Ruidoso in southwestern New Mexico. The oldest of four children, she had been given the responsibility of her younger sister Cindy, who had an undiagnosed brain disorder that left her subject to frequent seizures. Jennifer was the family member who advocated for Cindy, found her appropriate living arrangements, visited her regularly, and, over holidays, brought Cindy to wherever she was living. In 1973, Jennifer was all of twenty-six, and she had already been caring for Cindy for years. Jennifer was a tough cookie. A little taller than me with fair skin and light brown hair, she had blue eyes that alternately sparkled with joy and flashed with anger. Outside of Meg, she was my most trusted comrade.

Helaine Harris and Lee Schwing, also from The Furies collective, came to that meeting. Jennifer's new lover, Kate Winter, was also interested, as were four women from Ann Arbor who had just moved to DC, and who Meg and I met at the bar one night—Judy Dlugacz, Sue Sasser, Cindy Gair, and Carol Ginsberg. We just talked about possibilities. It might have been Helaine who proposed getting into video production, but the equipment was very expensive and the learning curve too daunting. Judy wanted to start a feminist restaurant but I didn't think that would have the impact I was hoping for, and what was I going to write? Menus?

We kept meeting and Meg kept performing.

Meg spent a lot of time in record stores, looking for songs that she could cover. One day she discovered an album by Garn Littledyke in the bargain bin. The album was called *Wichita Lineman* and on the cover was a straight but tough-looking woman leaning against a telephone pole. Meg could hardly contain her excitement—had she found an unknown lesbian singer on a major label? Alas, Garn Littledyke was a man. But Meg's bargain bin hunting was not always fruitless. That's where she first discovered Cris Williamson.

Cris had recorded an album for Ampex shortly before Ampex stopped producing records. The record went nowhere commercially, but it went right into Meg's heart and repertoire. One song in particular—"Joanna"—got her attention. "Joanna" was a song about female friendship and caring that didn't follow the usual verse-chorus-verse-chorus formula, and that made it musically interesting. Meg began performing it regularly and always credited Cris as the songwriter. And so it was that when, in the spring of 1973, Cris made her first trip to the DC area for a concert at a coffeehouse on the campus of American University, the room was filled with women—women who knew of Cris because Meg had been singing her songs and promoting the gig. Cris started in on "Joanna" but almost immediately forgot some of the words. She was visibly shocked when half the audience started filling in the words and singing the song.

> Get down off the ceiling, Joanna
> Let's sit and talk for a while

It's been so long since I've seen you
And I really need to see you smile.

....

We don't have to speak necessarily
A smile would be just fine with me
But you're on another level and I wonder how you are
How are you these days?

Are you alright? Do you sleep at night?
Do you have enough time to use your mind?
Do you remember your own name?
I don't know the places you're into.

Meg and Cris performing together for the first
time, at the DC Women's Center

After the concert, Meg introduced herself to Cris and asked her what she thought about Women's Music. By now Cris had heard of Meg—apparently dozens of women had told her that Meg Christian was singing some of her songs. But Cris didn't have a clue about Women's Music. Of course not. Meg had just invented the term. Meg handed her a tape she had made and invited Cris to dinner at our house.

Meg and I were nervous wrecks as we prepared for the dinner. We so wanted to impress Cris, and there was so much about her that was impressive to us—she wrote her own songs, she had recorded an album, she had a gorgeous, wide-ranging voice, she came from California. All these things were a bit intimidating to me. Meg was hoping to find a musical kindred spirit. We didn't even know if she was a lesbian. On the one hand, there were no references to men in any of her songs. She performed in pants. She exuded what we were hoping was a lesbian vibe. On the other hand, she had long hair that she was forever flipping back. And she arrived at our house with her manager, a guy named Peter.

Cris and Peter arrived late, and we were not pleased to see him. We thought she was using Peter as a shield. We didn't know how we would be able to talk to her about feminism and lesbianism with Peter there. We all tried to cover our anxiety in our own ways. Meg drank a lot of wine. I acted tough and disinterested. Cris immediately started doing yoga poses on the living room floor. Within five minutes she was doing shoulder stands and planks and lunges. I don't think we had ever seen anyone do yoga before. She talked about energy and vibes. Cris kept saying that in California the leash was a little longer than in Washington, DC. We thought she was one of the strangest people we had ever met. We hung out for several hours, eyeing each other warily, and talking about nothing of consequence.

We made a tuna noodle casserole for dinner, which was something we ate pretty regularly. We didn't want Cris to think we were anything but cool, so we didn't want to appear to be trying to impress her. We definitely succeeded in not impressing her, and the tuna noodle casserole later became the butt of much joking from the stage by both Meg and Cris.

Just a few weeks after that bizarre dinner, we met up again with Cris. Our friends Chris James and Shirl Smith were part of a feminist radio collective called Sophie's Parlor, which broadcast from the radio station at Georgetown University. When Chris and Shirl decided to interview Cris Williamson, they invited Meg and me to participate in the interview. So, on a spring afternoon in 1973, we all piled into the small studio at WGTB and found our places around the table. Mics were set up and adjusted. The interview began in a low-key fashion with some typical questions about how long she had been performing, how did she write, etc. After we all loosened up a bit, we started making jokes about women's tap dance companies and women's puppet shows. We asked Cris about her experience with Ampex and she spoke of how frustrating it was for her to have had so little control of the process of making the record. And then she said, "Why don't you start a women's record company?" And that was it. I knew immediately what I was going to do. I did not have one second of doubt.

After that, I talked to everyone I knew about starting a women's record company and invited them all to join. The ten of us who had met in January showed up, and Meg and I presented the case for a record company. By the end of the meeting, we had agreed. On that night, and over the next few months, we began to outline a set of basic principles that would guide us. We created a set of documents elucidating our vision, our strategy, and some rules of the game.

The preamble said,

> This record company was started by Lesbian feminists
> to provide a means of equalizing economic/cultural
> inequalities which exist in this country. We believe
> that women, and therefore lesbians, are oppressed by
> the heterosexual and capitalistic institutions already in
> existence and we are committed to finding ways, within
> the company, of alleviating class, race, and heterosexual
> privilege.
>
> Because women have been denied the means of
> communicating their music and their culture, we intend
> to seek out and encourage women's musical achieve-
> ments. Finally, we are committed to producing quality
> recordings of quality music.

We listed all the departments, how they would function, how
they would interact with each other, how women would be
hired and fired. We established a grievance procedure, a salary
structure, a method for handling disputes. We insisted that all
meetings would be held during regular working hours, and that
all financial records would be accessible to everyone.

We would operate collectively. We would work exclusively
with women. We would treat all women with respect. We would
record music that celebrated all aspects of women's lives. We
would operate with transparency. We would not create a hier-
archy or star system—we believed that all work was valuable
and should be equally compensated and honored. We wanted to
create an alternative economic institution that would eventually
enable us to control all the means of production and to employ
hundreds or thousands of women in well-paying jobs, doing
meaningful work, with opportunities to learn new skills and to
become part of the decision-making collective. We would be as
non-capitalistic as possible. We believed we were acting with

integrity from a set of feminist values that we all subscribed to and were living to the best of our abilities. I believed that we would create a model for feminism that would be irresistible. "This is what feminism looks like? I want in."

It never crossed our minds that knowing nothing about making records would be a problem.

There were feminist monthly newsletters in almost every city in the US, and in many small towns as well, and we had access to them because of our work with *The Furies*. We sent notices to all of them that essentially said, "We are starting a women's record company and if anybody knows anything about any aspect of this, please let us know." We also decided to go directly to the source. I wrote letters to four or five of the major record labels: "I am a high school student and I have to write a paper on how to start a record company. Can you please tell me what to do?" We actually got replies, although they were completely useless—"you need a million dollars, so forget about it," or, "it's too complicated to explain, so find another project."

Meanwhile, I was booking concerts for Meg for the summer of 1973, and we planned a cross-country trip that would end in the fabled state of California. Using the feminist press and the mailing list of subscribers from *The Furies* and DC's feminist monthly *off our backs*, I approached women everywhere and asked if they would produce a concert of Women's Music. The interest and willingness were immediate and extraordinary. Almost nobody had production experience, but that was irrelevant. I barely knew anything myself; however, I was one step ahead of them: find a hall and book it, print up some posters and plaster them wherever women hang out, sell tickets. Theatrical lighting was a plus, but if the best we could do was keep a row of overhead lights on the stage and lower the rest of the house, that would work.

I would run the sound. We packed the car and hit the road, unaware of what a great—and fortuitous—adventure this trip would turn out to be.

5 STRANGE PARADISE

Becoming a Record
Company, Sort Of

W HAT TO CALL THIS CREATION of ours? I'm sure we spent several meetings discussing the name for our new national women's record company. I remember suggesting Rutherford Records, in honor of the great British actor Margaret Rutherford, who portrayed the smart and independent Miss Marple in the movies based on Agatha Christie's novels. Fortunately, that idea went nowhere. Another suggestion was Siren Records, implying both meanings of the word: the sirens on emergency vehicles with their message of "get out of the way, here we come," and the Sirens of Greek mythology ,whose beautiful music lured men to their deaths. Thankfully that was another idea that did not go far. Then Meg suggested Olivia. She had just read a novel called *Olivia* by a woman using the pseudonym Olivia. We later learned the author was Dorothy Strachey. *Olivia* told the story of a young woman's infatuation with the headmistress of her boarding school and her observation of the headmistress's tense love affair with the other female head of the school. We decided we liked it. Olivia. A woman's name, a lesbian story, and it was such a round sound, it rolled off the tongue. It was mellifluous. Perfect for a Women's Music company.

Kate designed an Art Deco logo with "Olivia" in shades of burgundy and lavender. We rented a PO Box, Kate designed letterhead, and we were official.

Olivia's new logo, designed by Kate Winter

We had heard that Kate Millett, a brilliant feminist writer, artist, and activist—the author of *Sexual Politics*—had produced an outdoor music festival with all women performers in Sacramento. We got a list of musicians who had performed and set out at the end of June on our first cross-country tour—to find as many of them as we could.

We drove all day, every day, stopping for picnic lunches and finding campgrounds to land in before dark. We were nervous campers, neither of us having ever done it before. We stayed mostly in KOA campgrounds, which had showers and toilets and lots of other campers and signs warning us not to leave food out because of the bears. We became slightly obsessed with the bears and would be washing our dishes and locking our food up in the car almost before we had finished eating. We never did see any bears, which was both a relief and a disappointment.

But once we got to the West Coast, we did encounter some amazing beings who would have a huge impact on how we set our course. In Berkeley, we met Willyce Kim. Willyce was a poet whose first book, *Eating Artichokes,* had been published in 1972 by the Oakland Women's Press Collective. Willyce introduced us to Subie Baker. Subie worked at Leopold's, a big independent record store on Durant Ave., just above Telegraph and right next to Tower Records—which was a big West Coast chain. Subie was a fount of information about how record stores operate and how records get into record stores. Since we knew nothing about any aspect of the recording business, we had assumed that we would distribute our records the way everyone else did, whatever that was. Subie had another idea. We should avoid the established distributors, the one-stops, the men who exercised so much control over which records got precious space in stores. We should set up our own distribution network, using women all over the country. Willyce and Subie offered to be our Berkeley distributors. They were the first. How perfect was that?

Meg and I called home, full of excitement about this discovery and the incredible enthusiasm women were expressing, mostly having heard about this new women's record company through the feminist press. In fact, during this call we learned that someone had actually written to Olivia in answer to our plea for information on how to do what we were doing. The letter was from Joan Lowe, who lived in Vida, Oregon. Joan had her own record label, Pacific Cascade, under which she produced and recorded children's records. We looked at our maps and saw that Vida was pretty far out of our way, but we thought, okay, we'll stop by for an hour or two and see what she has to say.

In 1973, the town of Vida wasn't much more than a small post office and a little grocery store. Joan lived in a small cabin on the Mackenzie River, surrounded by huge fir trees, at the base of the Pacific Cascade Mountains. We pulled onto her land at around noon and heard what sounded like a dozen ferocious dogs barking. As we walked toward the cabin, we felt some trepidation, and not just because of the dogs. Her letter to Olivia was very stiff and formal. She lived alone in the woods. What would she do when she learned we were lesbians?

One look at Joan and we knew we didn't have to worry about the lesbian part. She was instantly recognizable with her short, dark hair combed back in a DA, her butchy sweater, and her jeans. We shook hands and she introduced us to Angelique, the very sweet Rottweiler who loved to watch Westerns on TV because she liked seeing the horses, and Signe, the Swedish jämthund (who looked very much like a well-groomed, well-fed wolf). Joan was as nervous as we were. There was nothing hip or cool about Joan. She was already in her forties and looked and acted like someone from another generation. She was deeply closeted, very reserved, not part of a feminist community, and not involved in movement politics. But she was passionate about the land, and the river, and keeping the town of Vida alive.

Once the dogs calmed down and finished sniffing us and licking our hands, we began to feel the peace of Joan's home. It was a beautiful August day, the sky a clear, deep blue. Joan had the back doors open, and we could hear the river rushing and the wind in the trees.

Still, since Meg and I didn't have much time to spend in Oregon, we wanted to get right to it, and Joan was a pretty no-nonsense person herself. She was intrigued by our dreams and plans and fascinated with the community of women that we were a part of. She let us see her wicked sense of humor and her longing for connection. Within an hour, she was pouring wine and defrosting lamb chops, and we were figuring out where we could sleep so we could spend the night.

We talked for hours. We had finally met the person who could tell us how to be a record company. She knew every aspect of the business, so we began to learn a new vocabulary: 4-track, 8-track, mastering, test pressing, acetate, mechanicals, etc. We talked about the actual physical label that went on each vinyl record and how to design them, and that each record we produced needed its own catalog number. Catalog number! That meant we would have a catalog! We were jumping out of our skin. We decided our first record, whatever it was, would be LF 901. LF for Lesbian Feminist; 901 because there were ten of us. She suggested that instead of a whole album, our first record should be a 45-rpm single. In those days, a hit single was the key to a well-selling album. But for us, it would be a great way to begin and to learn more about all the parts of the operation of which we were basically ignorant. We loved the idea. She said, "Let's start."

She had turned her living room into a 4-track recording studio, with mics and mic stands, big reel-to-reel machines, and all kinds of filters and sound enhancers that we knew nothing about. She sent the dogs outside, closed the glass doors and windows that faced the river, and suddenly we were in a sound-proof room. After a couple of glasses of wine, Meg was ready. She decided to record "Robbery," which she had been performing for a while. Written by Sally Piano (later Sirani Avedis) the song was an angry paean to suffering and revolution. Meg did a couple of takes and finally nailed it. She had the passion and the conviction. She made the song her own. But in the end, Sally would not allow Olivia to release the recording. (She felt that Meg had not actually suffered enough in her life to be worthy.) But in that moment of recording—in Vida, Oregon, with our new friend and savior Joan Lowe at the controls and Meg at the mic, we were ecstatic.

Joan Lowe getting ready to record Meg in her studio in Vida, OR

Once we got back to DC, the other Olives, as we called ourselves, immediately saw the wisdom of starting with a 45. We had no intention of selling it. We would use it as a fund-raiser—press a few hundred copies and send them out to women in the music industry who we thought would be sympathetic, and anyone else who we thought would be supportive enough to send some money. We wanted to establish ourselves as a national women's record company and not the label of a single musician, and therefore we thought it best if we had Meg on one side and someone else on the other.

This was especially important to me because I was primarily interested in building a political movement; the music and the record company were a means to that end. I truly believed that the path to getting women marching, organizing, demanding their rights went directly through their hearts. The music was the means. Feminist revolution was the end. I was crazy in love with Meg and thought she was a perfect embodiment of all our values. I wanted her to make our first record. But, still, I did not want Olivia to be Meg's record company. It had to be bigger than that.

And so we asked Cris to sing something for the other side of the 45, and she readily agreed. By this time, we were becoming friends. Cris and Meg had performed together in DC—their first concert was in March 1973, a benefit for Radio Free Women. Cris was now staying at our house when she came to DC. One of the fabulous pieces of furniture in our otherwise oddly furnished house was a player piano. Though there were dozens of old piano rolls in the basement, we rarely played them. We did use the piano a lot—Cris and Meg would play songs for each other, working out parts with Cris playing piano and Meg on guitar.

We invited Cris to play some songs for us at an Olivia collective meeting so we could decide which one we wanted for the 45. As soon as she played "If It Weren't for the Music," we knew that was the one. Like many of her songs, it had an unusual musical structure—not just verse/chorus/verse/chorus—and the words were perfect, opening with:

Well if it weren't for the music
Bringing us together in a natural way
I'd still be looking for a way to say
I want to be your good friend

....

I know that when I look at you
It makes me high
And like a songbird you've got me soaring in circles
Singing my heart out
You make me fly

We asked Cris to donate her performance and she said that as long was Meg was donating hers, she would too. By this time we knew that Meg would not be allowed to record Sally Piano's song "Robbery." Eventually she chose "Lady," written by Carole King and Gerry Goffin. The song addresses a woman, asking her to think about what she has given up and lost for the sake of the man she is with, and whether it was worth it.

Joan agreed to fly out and be our recording engineer and all she asked for was her expenses. She told me what to look for in booking a studio, and for us, price was a huge consideration. I opened the Yellow Pages and started calling. I felt like I was speaking a foreign language, asking the questions Joan had told me to ask, about tracks and outboard equipment and limiters, and also, most importantly, whether we could bring in our own engineer. Several places I spoke to were skeptical about a woman engineer and I moved on. Eventually I found Omega. They said they had what we wanted, they were fine with having Joan do the recording, and the price was right. I booked some hours.

On October 16th, 1973, Cris went into the studio and one hour later we had a finished song. Then it was Meg's turn. She was very nervous about her session. Her only previous studio experience was as part of a chorus for a radio commercial and she was a little intimidated by the ease with which Cris laid down her tracks. She needed numerous takes, but when our studio time was up, she was not satisfied. After Cris and Joan had gone back to the West Coast, Meg followed and, in Joan's studio on the Mackenzie River, she finally got a version she was happy with. Now we had the makings of our first record.

I still had my teaching job, but whenever I could, I would join Meg on the road. Meg was writing more songs and starting to perform them. She debuted "Ode to a Gym Teacher" on September 21 at the DC Women's Center.

> I wrote her name on my note-pad
> And I inked it on my dress
> And I etched it on my locker
> And I carved it on my desk
> And I painted big red hearts with her initials
> on my books
> And I never knew 'til later why I got those
> funny looks.

Having a crush on your high school gym teacher was almost a rite of passage for lesbians in those days. For me, it was Miss Carly. I used to walk home from school going blocks out of my way in order to walk by her house, hoping that she would see me and invite me in, but also hoping she would not see me because I would not know what to say to her. I was not alone in this. Women simply howled with delight when Meg talked about her beloved Miss Berger and then sang this song.

Meanwhile, the Olivia collective members were getting ready to be a record company. We had to take care of the licensing for "Lady," get the music from tape to acetate to test pressing to vinyl, design the label, and accomplish all the tasks of running a small business, like setting up a bookkeeping system and opening a bank account. Some of these we knew how to do. Others, we did not, but we always managed to find someone to help. My mother, for example, gave me a quick refresher course in the basics of bookkeeping—assets and liabilities, debits and credits, and how to enter items into the ledgers.

We also had to raise money. We made a list of every woman we thought would be supportive of a women's record label and would be willing and able to donate large amounts of money. Knowing nothing at all about the art of fundraising, we crafted a letter in which we laid out the bleak landscape for women in the music business—how they had neither control over their music and careers nor power in the industry; how they were put in boxes and not allowed to break out; and how that resulted in wasted talent, unfulfilled dreams, and an audience of women frustrated by a culture that did not reflect their lives. We followed that with our vision of Olivia. We wanted to tantalize them with the possibilities that a woman-identified, boldly feminist music company could mean for them and for all women. We talked about women as recording engineers, record producers, instrumentalists. What could they envision for themselves if they were able to make all the decisions about what songs to record, which musicians to work with, how to shape the sound, what art should grace the album cover, how the artist and the album should be promoted? We also talked about the importance of building feminist institutions that would demonstrate the *real* meaning of feminism (as opposed to how the mainstream media defined it) on a daily basis. And then we asked them to make a donation.

The letter went out to dozens and dozens of people—Joni Mitchell, Judy Collins, Merry Clayton, Dusty Springfield, Carole King, Helen Reddy, Aretha Franklin, Carly Simon, Anne Murray, Donna Summer, Jackson Brown, James Taylor,

Linda Ronstadt, Bette Midler, Olivia Newton-John, Patti LaBelle, Barbara Streisand, Gloria Steinem, Robin Morgan, Flo Kennedy, Bella Abzug, Shulamith Firestone, Aileen Hernandez, Karen DeCrow, Maya Angelou, members of our family... Other than our family members, we had addresses for none of them. All we had were the names and addresses of their record labels or management companies or publishers or national organizations. I would guess that almost none of our letters ever made it to the women we sent them to, with three exceptions. A musician named Harriet Schock, who was recording on a major label at that time and was happy to support our fledgling operation, sent $25. Meg's uncle sent $50. And Yoko Ono sent an invitation to meet with her.

Yoko Ono. We didn't know very much about her except that her music was like nothing we had ever heard before. It was very dissonant and, if there were lyrics, they were incomprehensible to us. The other thing we knew about her was that she was married to John Lennon and so probably had a lot of money. She was doing a performance at the Smithsonian Museum in January 1974 and asked us to come to her hotel room before the show and meet with her.

Nobody in the collective now remembers this, but I know that I went to see Yoko and I'm pretty sure Meg came with me. All of us met for hours trying to figure out how best to approach her. There was no Internet, so no way to Google her and get background. In the end, we just decided to be direct. We also decided we had better dress up, which meant wearing pants other than jeans and possibly even putting on a bra. But possibly not.

We tried to act very cool, but I was quite nervous. As much as I didn't want to admit it, I couldn't stop thinking that this woman was married to one of the Beatles. I had no idea who she was in her own right. We went up to her room and she opened the door with a smile. She was so small! Her dark hair was pulled back in a ponytail and she wore loose, patterned pants and a blousy, artsy top. We introduced ourselves.

"Welcome," she said, holding out her hand. "Please come in. Would you like some tea?"

"Yes please," said Meg at the same moment that I said, "No thank you." We rolled our eyes at each other. I felt so clumsy.

She pulled a brown cigarette out of a pack with a French name that I had never heard of. I pulled out my pack of Marlboros, relieved that I wouldn't have to get through this without smoking. Yoko poured a cup of tea for Meg and we sat down. She had draped pieces of fabric on the boxy hotel furniture and made it seem warmer and softer. She kept the curtains closed but had candles lit. The impression was of being in a cave, or a womb. There was a slight whiff of incense— enough to suggest a mood, but not enough to overwhelm. We sat uncomfortably on a stiff sofa while she sat in a wingback chair.

She looked directly at us and almost whispered, "Tell me your ideas." Meg and I launched into our story. Yoko listened intently. "Yes, I know how badly women are treated in the music business. I am full of creativity and I am not taken seriously. I would like to help you."

Feeling emboldened now, I said we needed money so that we could make our first record. Would she make a donation?

"I will not give you money but I will be happy to give you one of my songs, and to record it for you and you can sell it."

What a stunning offer. An offer that we were completely unprepared to accept. How could we possibly fit the music of Yoko Ono into our idea of Women's Music? Who would buy a record with her music on it? Did this have even the slightest chance of feeding women's hunger, or building a foundation for a feminist institution? We told her that we already had contracted with two musicians for our first record and thank you very much anyway. "Let me know if you change your mind," she said as she got up to show us out. "I have respect for what you want to do." And then we left.

We really had no idea why she was reaching out to us. We were so wrapped up in our own story that we didn't pay attention to hers, to see where there was common ground. Yoko Ono was an outsider, commercially not viable, too anti-establishment. The music press and Beatles' fans blamed her for breaking up the Beatles. She was considered a joke and a harridan by the male music establishment.

In retrospect it's easy to see what we had missed in potential connections, but I think it was actually the right decision. We needed our first statement to be more directly and intimately linked to the feminist and lesbian feminist movement. We wanted our artists to tour as part of the concert production network we were beginning to establish around the country. And we wanted music that was more accessible than Yoko's was, especially at that time. But because she didn't offer us what we wanted, we dismissed her and never looked back.

On February 14, 1974, Meg and I celebrated Valentine's Day. I had asked her what she wanted her gift to be and she told me she wanted a new apron. And that's what she got. Then she sat me down in the living room and played her gift to me: "Valentine Song."

> It was once only dining and dancing
> Evening kisses, morning smiles
> And then you said, "Let's go off together
> Alone for a while"
>
> And I loved you at first for your wicked eyes
> And the laughter that loosens your bones

And your soft curls
And the passions that I've never known…

………

Yes, we bargained for doubtful tomorrows
But our past grows richer each day
And more and more, I cannot see me going away
With happiness here for our taking
Resting easy, feeling strong
As I delight in the life that we're making
I sing you this valentine song.

I could not look at Meg. I was afraid I would burst into tears, my heart overflowing with love, and I DID NOT CRY. My lover wrote a love song for me. To me. I was just a little short of ecstatic and a little nervous, too. I thought of myself as a behind-the-scenes person and was a little uncomfortable with the idea that women would start to look at me and know more about me than I was ready to tell them. That was about to change, and, the truth is, I loved having "Valentine Song" be Meg's public declaration of her love for me.

Whenever Meg and I traveled, we talked about Olivia. I began to do a short monologue right before the last song of Meg's first set. At first, I would just let women know that we had started the record company and something about our dreams and our plans. Eventually, I used the time to solicit distributors and donors and to encourage people to buy records. At first I talked about the 45 as a fundraising tool for our first album, which would be Meg's. When it became clear that our "rich people's mailing list" was not going to produce the desired results, if for no other reason than we didn't know how to reach anyone on it, we had to rethink our strategy. In addition, women let us know that it would not be acceptable to have recordings

Meg and me in our living room in DC

of Meg and Cris and not make them available to the public. So we decided we would sell the 45.

We sent out letters to everyone who had contacted us about Olivia, plus all the lists we had from the various feminist and lesbian newspapers, and we put announcements in all those papers as well. The record went on sale on May 11, 1974. We sold it for $1.50 plus 30¢ in postage and handling, and we left a space on the order blank for people to make an additional donation. (This was before the time of PayPal and MP3s and digital anything). Almost everyone included a donation. Some were 20¢, for a nice round $2 check. Several women sent $100; at least one sent $1,000. This was beyond our wildest dreams. Women were hungry, and we were beginning to feed them.

Of course, we were not alone. Other lesbian artists were starting labels and making records. "Lavender Jane Loves Women"—led by Alix Dobkin and Kay Gardner—had been released in November 1973. Maxine Feldman had recorded and released a 45 of her own "Angry Athis." Still, this did not constitute a glut of woman-identified music. And one of the things that distinguished us was we were intent on using the music to build institutions that would support a movement.

6 WHERE DO WE GO FROM HERE?

California Calls

UMMER OF 1974. OLIVIA WAS not yet two years old and already there were so many changes. Carol Ginsburg and Sue Sasser had decided that starting a women's record company was not for them, and they left to pursue other dreams. Jennifer and Kate were hired by the University of New Mexico to teach a class on feminism and they moved to Albuquerque, although they remained committed to Olivia and planned to be a part of whatever we did. Judy Dlugacz, who I expected to be the next to leave, dropped the first of several surprises in our laps one evening in December.

I had received a notice about a six-month class in recording engineering to be held in DC starting in February. I was already feeling burdened by the amount of Olivia business I was carrying, but I felt that one of us should take this class and become conversant with the language and basic principles and tools of this technical aspect of our work. I was afraid it was going to be me.

To this point, Judy had hardly participated. She was twenty, with dark hair, parted in the middle, that came to her shoulders. Originally from New York, she had gone to college in Ann Arbor, Michigan, and moved to DC with the intention of going to law school, but she got sidetracked and never made it. I didn't know her well; she didn't say much in meetings, and she didn't take on much of the work.

At the end of one of our regular collective meetings, I mentioned the recording class and asked if anyone was interested. Judy cleared her throat.

"I would like to do this," she said.

"What happened to law school?" I asked.

"I don't know about law school anymore. But I would like to learn recording. And I think Joan would mentor me too."

I was both relieved and skeptical. Would she really come through? I also noticed a twinge of reluctance on my part about letting go of this aspect of our work. Developing the ability to get sound onto tape seemed like such a crucial skill, and I wasn't entirely sure I trusted anybody other than myself to hold it. But in the end, I was glad I did. Judy took the class and also let Joan teach her. She learned to assist Joan in a variety of ways. Judy started taking over much of the technical work of Olivia and over time I learned to trust her judgement and rely on her expertise.

Now it was June. School was out, and Meg and I were preparing for another drive across the country. The 45 was out and was introducing Meg to a whole new group of women who wanted a concert in their town; new women's production groups were forming, some just for that purpose. In some cases, existing groups saw Women's Music concerts as a way to reach more women for their other feminist political work and as a way to make some money. I had no trouble booking a multi-city tour.

We had another big reason for going on the road. We wanted to meet with the leaders of some of the organizations in the lesbian and feminist community in Los Angeles. We were starting to think that Washington, DC, was not the ideal location for a lesbian feminist record company. Although DC was a hotbed of feminist organizing and activity, the music scene was not very well developed, and more than that, almost everything we needed to be a record company was located in New York, Nashville, or LA. Mastering labs, pressing plants, album jacket fabricators, even cardboard mailers for the 45s—none of that was available in DC. Would LA be a better place to be? And would the women's community of LA welcome us or consider us interlopers and carpetbaggers? We needed to find out.

Meg's concerts were now bringing in enough money that our travel style could move up a notch, and we went from KOA campgrounds (usually $3.50 a night) to Motel 6—costing $6.00 a night. Motel 6's reputation now is for grunge and sleaze, but in 1974 they were clean and had the added attraction of vibrating beds. Put a quarter in, lie down, and get a ten-minute massage. Instead of cooking every night over our Coleman stove, we went to diners or, for a really big treat, got take-out from Kentucky Fried Chicken, brought it back to our room, watched TV, and ate in bed.

Now that we had a product to sell, my raps during Meg's shows expanded. I still talked about our vision for Olivia, but I added a sales pitch and a plug for distributors. We sold hundreds of 45s, collected hundreds of names for our mailing list, and connected with dozens of new distributors. We met one of them when we got to Albuquerque.

Sandra L. (for Lesbian) Ramsey was a white, working-class woman—tall, thin, and with a strong opinion about everything. She was at the lesbian bar in Albuquerque where Meg performed in the summer of 1973 and was immediately taken with Meg's music and Olivia's politics. She had lots of lesbian friends who felt put off by the feminist movement; inside the Albuquerque feminist movement, she was the only out lesbian. Meeting Jennifer and Kate—strong and out lesbians—was a revelation for her.

They asked Sandy if she would be interested in being an Olivia distributor. Sandy hated sales, but she signed up because she believed in what we were doing. She eventually took over sales in most of New Mexico and did a great job until she moved to Los Angeles to join the collective.

Meg and I continued on our journey, stopping at some magnificent National Parks along the way. We spent a day roaming around the Painted Desert and the Petrified Forest in Arizona, and for over an hour we were the only human beings on the trail. The colors and the shapes of mesas and the mounds were astonishing. I had never seen anything like it. "Awesome" is such an overused word now, but this land was truly awesome, sedate and wild at the same time.

We went from stark nature, few people, and extreme quiet to Los Angeles. The transition might have been harder if we hadn't been *so* excited to get to LA. We were hoping to find our future here. We met with women from *The Lesbian Tide*, Sisterhood Books, and the LA Women's Building. We met with women who were producing shows at bars and others who were thinking about starting women's businesses. The meetings went well; everyone seemed excited that Olivia might become a part of their community and encouraged us to move. We sent letters and cassette tapes about our meetings and our impressions to our comrades in DC, letting them know that we were starting to lean towards California.

We drove north to Santa Barbara to meet with Margie Adam, a wonderful pianist who had performed at the music festival in Sacramento organized by Kate Millett. Margie was beginning to make her mark as a songwriter and performer on the suddenly sprouting Women's Music circuit, which was yet another outgrowth of the extraordinary amount of creative energy unleashed by the Women's and Lesbian Liberation Movements.

We weren't quite sure what to make of Margie when she opened the door. She seemed warm and also reserved. She was tall and thin, with a full head of brown curls perfectly placed. She had the kind of erect posture I associated with finishing schools where the girls were required to walk around with books on their heads. Even her pressed, blue denim overalls and long-sleeve, plaid cotton shirt had an elegance about them. Margie was originally from Lompoc, a small, mostly white town about an hour north and west of Santa Barbara. Her father had owned the daily newspaper in Lompoc, and her mother was a classical pianist. Margie had started playing piano as soon as she could climb onto the bench. Her posture at the piano was also impeccable.

The first amazing experience we had at Margie's was seeing an avocado tree with dozens of actual avocados on it. Who knew that avocados grew on trees, and you could grow one in your own front yard? California was looking more and more appealing. The second amazing experience was watching and listening to Margie and Meg make music together, Margie on piano, Meg on guitar or autoharp. One would start playing a song—which the other had never heard before—and within a few bars the other would be adding parts. When Margie added a line of ascending chords to Meg's version of "Hello Hooray," I thought I would jump out of my skin. Adding a bass line to the song—leading up to the line "I've been waiting so long"—gave it so much more poignancy and power. I took about twenty-five photos of them playing this song together, hoping I could capture some of the magic on film.

"Hello Hooray" was written by Rolf Kempf, and Meg had heard it on a Judy Collins record. It had become the song with which she opened her concerts and would be the first song on her first album. As she did with so many songs that men wrote,

Meg and Margie Adam working out parts for "Hello Hooray."
You can almost see the avocado tree through the window.

Meg changed some of the words so that the song would center on women and women's experiences. She sang it like this:

Hello hooray
Let the show begin
I'm ready

Hello hooray
Let the lights grow dim
We've been ready

Ready for the rain to fall
Just to fall again
Ready for a woman to be born
Only to be born again, and again, and
        again, and again

        ....

I've been waiting so long for another song
I've been thinking so long I was the only one
We've been hoping so long for another song

        ....

After all these years of crying
And self-denying
And lonely waiting
And fears and hesitating
Yes we'll laugh, yes we'll laugh, and we'll laugh
As we see this thing
Finally, finally, finally begin,
And begin, and begin.

We knew right away that we would want Margie to come to
DC to play on Meg's album. We wanted her to record her part
on this song, and, it turned out, on others as well.

Back in LA we'd been invited to a concert that a young
woman named Vicki Randle was giving in a small LA club.

Women in the business were starting to know about us and wanted to get themselves in front of us in the hopes of landing a recording contract. Vicki's manager was very much a part of the mainstream music industry, and she had told Vicki to play to us at the show, making lots of eye contact and winking at us, which we found extremely bizarre and uncomfortable. Were we supposed to be acting like record company executives? I felt like I should be smoking a cigar. Vicki had a voice like honey—so smooth and rich—and an ability to put heart into a song. She played acoustic guitar and sang covers of pop music. At one point, she sang Joni Mitchell's "Free Man in Paris" and was sending signals to us through the song, but I had no idea what they meant. Was she trying to tell us she was a lesbian? After her set, she sat with us at our table. She was extraordinarily shy and once off the stage could barely make eye contact, but after we had some drinks and loosened up and stopped trying to impress each other, we found we liked her.

Cris had come down to LA from her home in Northern California, and soon the five of us—Cris, Vicki, Margie, Meg and me—were hanging out. It was a magical time. Meg and I were clear that we would be back. We knew we would have some convincing to do with the rest of the collective, but LA had everything we thought we needed to really launch Olivia. On our last day in Los Angeles, the five of us met for breakfast at a diner. We dragged it out as long as we could and then walked outside to say our final goodbyes. We had a group hug around a parking meter, and we looked down and noticed the little red flag was up and the meter's message was "Time Expired." And so it was. Meg and I got in the car and started back to DC.

Once we were home, our first collective meeting was full of surprises. Meg and I were so excited about every aspect of the trip and about the possibilities we saw. The LA women's community was ready to open their arms to us. There was so much more music happening there and so many more opportunities for women musicians to perform. LA was one of the centers of the recording industry, so we wouldn't have to send halfway across the country just to get record mailers, and we would be able to hand-carry our finished tapes through all the steps to the pressing plant. We would be closer to Joan Lowe and Cris. Plus—avocado trees! We were sure the rest of the Olives would want to join us. Kate and Jennifer had already said they would.

I noticed as we were laying out the case that Helaine, Lee, and Cindy Gair (one of the four women who had recently moved to DC from Ann Arbor) would not look at us, and only gave sideways looks to each other. Cindy spoke first. "You know, while you were gone, we had to do all the things here that you usually do. It's a lot."

Then Helaine said, "And there's so much work and time tied up in shipping out records—and we only have one little record. Wouldn't it make sense to set something up where we could be shipping out lots of stuff? Women's stuff? Books, records, crafts—all the stuff women are making."

Apparently they had worked out their lines for us. Lee was next. "We agree with you completely. Olivia should be in LA. But we don't want to move."

Helaine again: "We want to start a women's distribution company, and we want all the Olivia records to be part of it. We want to work with all the women who have signed up to be Olivia distributors, add more where we need them, and create a network to get all this great lesbian and feminist art out. What do you think?"

What did I think? I thought it was a bad idea. I was angry because, outside of coming to meetings, I didn't think these three women had actually done much of the work of Olivia, and now, having spent two months doing the grunt work that

I did every day, they decided they didn't want to be a record company. I was angry because they wanted to take over the distributors, whom they had done nothing to recruit or train. I was hurt because they didn't share our enthusiasm, and they didn't seem any longer to share our vision.

I wanted to consult with Jennifer and Kate, but I was pretty sure we would reject their offer. I felt strongly that the distribution network was a critical piece of the whole picture. I wanted us to be in control of every aspect of our business. More than that, I saw the distributors as our representatives, our cadre in each city and town. I wanted all of us to be connected to each other—that was the revolutionary network I wanted to build.

Judy had been pretty quiet during this meeting, and I just assumed she would be staying in DC. But she provided the second surprise of the day when she said she would move to Los Angeles with us. And so, along with Jennifer and Kate, the Olivia collective was now five.

During the summer, we had set in motion the steps to make Meg's album. Now we really got down to work. The plan was to record in October 1974, have it ready for Christmas release, and move to LA in March 1975. We did record in October and we did move in March. But we could not release the album until we were in LA, and that's another story.

7 LIVE DREAM

Making *I Know You Know,* Our First Album

"**A**RE YOU TELLING ME THAT once Meg records 'Valentine Song,' anybody else in the world can record it?" I was frantic with disbelief and disgust. "Frank Sinatra could record it?"

Looking down as if she were personally responsible for this turn of affairs, Joan Lowe mumbled, "Afraid so. He would have to pay songwriter royalties, of course, but he could record it and sing it wherever and whenever."

"So then how can Sally Piano keep Meg from recording 'Robbery'?" Jennifer asked, barely able to contain her outrage.

"Because Sally hasn't recorded the song. That's how it goes."

The Olivia collective, now down to the five women who would carry it forward—Jennifer Woodul, Kate Winter, Judy Dlugacz, Meg, and me—sat around Meg's and my living room on Carpenter Street with Joan and Cris Williamson. We were getting ready to record Meg's album. It was October 1974. Joan would be our recording engineer. Cris would co-produce with Meg, and together they would decide on the instrumentation for each song to back up Meg's vocals and guitar parts; identify, hire, and schedule the studio time for all the musicians; decide which of the many "takes" was the right one; work with Joan to mix all the sounds once recorded (e.g., boost the back-up vocals here, lose the piano part after the third bar, etc.); and determine the final order of songs for the record. But the first item on the agenda was selecting the songs, and we were all at least a little repulsed at the idea that a man could take one of Meg's precious songs—songs to women, songs from a woman's heart—and contaminate it with his maleness. "Valentine Song" was *my* song. Meg had written it for *me*. A lesbian love song. Not a heterosexual love song—the world already had enough of those. And Frank Sinatra, of all people, a known woman-izer who was reportedly physically abusive to his wives and girlfriends. Not that Frank Sinatra—or any other man—ever expressed any interest in "Valentine Song" or any other lesbian love song, but there was a principle here. We wanted to own what we created. We were not interested in ownership in the capitalistic sense. The Lesbian and Women's Movements were laying claim to our bodies, our sexuality, our new ways of being in the world, and now, our culture. To learn that a man could take our precious creation and make it his without even asking just seemed wrong. Yes, his record company would have to pay royalties, but no amount of money could compensate for the violation that we would feel.

We batted around the idea that Meg should never record her own compositions so that we could keep them out of male mouths, but in the end decided that would be self-defeating. She would record her songs and we would take our chances, and, if a man did record one of them, we would take the royalties and use them to make more lesbian feminist music. This was just another lesson about the difficulty of navigating a feminist path inside a patriarchal world.

We were going back to Omega, the studio we used to record the 45. The studio was not very high-tech or well-put-together, which is what made it affordable for us, but it meant that Joan had to crawl around on the floor every day and connect pieces of equipment to other pieces of equipment so that we could use all eight tracks. The control room was called that because all the sound was controlled at the board from there—volume, panning (whether a particular instrument would be heard more on the left, right, or center), effects like reverb and more. Behind Joan and Cris—and Meg, once she had laid down her guitar and vocal tracks—at the board was a row of tape recorders, each about five feet high, two feet wide and three feet deep, all controlled remotely from the board. In front of and below the board were a couple of chairs for guests, random visitors, and record company executives. That's where I sat almost every day. I suppose I was now in that category of "record company executive," but I sure didn't feel like one. As usual, I had no idea what I was doing, and, as usual, I just kept making it up. In fact, Olivia *was* becoming a record company. The 45 was not just a throw-away—a little taste of what might be possible—it was the prelude to what was possible, and we were really doing it. Meg and Cris had the music. Joan had the technology. I could provide almost everything else. Kate and Jennifer were still in New Mexico, and Judy had a full-time job.

So I sat in front of the board and watched the musicians through a pane of thick, slanted glass. This made the large room where the music was actually played soundproof, and it meant that in the control room we could talk without being heard by the musicians in the studio.

Many of the musicians we brought in to play on the album had no studio experience, and some were not professional musicians, but they were skilled at their instruments and Meg had strong personal connections to them. Lilli Vincenz was one of the string players, and part of a women's amateur string ensemble. Lilli was an early activist and one of the first women in the DC homophile movement, as it was known then. In 1965, along with other lesbians and gay men (including Frank Kameny, who co-founded the Mattachine Society), Lilli picketed the White House to demand civil rights for lesbians and gays. She was one of the first people Meg had come out to when she got to DC. Meg wanted Lilli to play on her album as a way to honor her, and she did well. Another instrumentalist started out as a stranger who was recommended by someone else, and she didn't really have the chops for the more complicated parts. She tried over and over and never really got what Cris and Meg wanted to hear. Some of the music was beautiful and some of the musicians were brilliant. But no matter how it went, everyone was supportive, everyone was willing to try one more time, everyone was kind. Nobody had a tantrum, nobody was insulting, nobody pulled a power trip on anyone else. Anneke Earhart, who played piano on the Linda Lewis song "Goodbye Joanna," wrote to Meg after we finished the album:

> Anyway I was on cloud nine for days after I was in the studio. I think that was one of the best times I have ever had. There is an incredible sense of power creating like that, on our own terms for ourselves. When I was doing my thing, my sense of listening and being was so acutely heightened, I mean it was either perfect or it wasn't, you know.... Most of the licks I came up with were parts of my repertoire that I figured out how to shape to your song and I had never done that before, and learned a great deal from doing that. Most important I guess is that the experience has sunk a hook into me to be really serious about being a musician, to find other women to work with.... I had always been scared to be really serious about it, to put myself on the line, to perform, to have that kind of commitment. And the strokes praise respect I got from you and others has made me feel like I can do it.

We had received a gift of $10,000 from a woman who believed in what we were doing. We had a little more money coming in from sales for the 45. I was trying to keep the budget for the entire project to $10,000. Ten thousand dollars for everything—studio time, paying musicians, royalties to all the songwriters, tape, photography for the album jacket, labels, jacket fabrication and printing, all the test pressings, actually pressing the vinyl, and advertising and promotion. With an initial pressing of 5,000 records, that would mean a cost of $2.00 per record. We wanted to retail them for $5.00, sell them direct to stores for $3.50 and sell them to our growing network of distributors for $3.00. The economics of this were pure lunacy, but, really, what about this project wasn't?

In any case, every day after I finished teaching school, I would head over to the studio to join Meg, Cris, Joan, and whoever was coming in that day to record. I would sit in the chair in front of the board and alternate being thrilled by what I was witnessing and freaked out by how much time it was taking. More time meant more money. Every day, I sat in my chair and re-worked the budget, trying to figure out how to make a $50,000 project cost $10,000. I was worried about Joan's ability to navigate the jury-rigged studio and whether she knew how to work in an 8-track studio and use all the effects. I was worried about Meg and whether she was really getting the album she wanted. I was worried about Cris and whether she had Meg's best interests at heart in her production decisions. I was worried about whether we would finish this album in time for a Christmas release, which was what we were hoping for and counting on. I did love watching my lover making music with her friends, and, when I wasn't in a state of anxiety, I was in ecstasy. But there were times when I was not so much fun to be around.

Cris was staying with us in our extra bedroom, and one morning, late in the process, she asked to talk to me privately, something she never did. I approached her with wariness. She put her arm through mine and walked me into her room, shutting the door behind her. "I want you to stay home for a few days. Don't come to the studio." She was not asking, but she was not pushing, either. "When you're there, you watch the clock. And Meg watches you watching the clock, but she needs to be in the music, not in the budget." Any doubts I had about Cris dissolved in that moment. It was not easy to make demands on me or to stand up to me. Cris knew I didn't really trust her. I had wanted her to come out on stage and I wanted her to be more overtly feminist and political. There was also what I thought of as her "Californianess"—she was so airy, and I was so earthy. She believed deeply in spirit, and I was a committed materialist. More than that, I was very protective of Meg and this record and the whole record company. This baby wasn't all mine, but I had a very big stake in it. I thought her telling me to stay home was incredibly brave, and she was letting me know that she was really shouldering her responsibility as album producer, that she wanted this record to be as good as it could be and that she was going to take care of Meg. I understood this immediately and felt enormously grateful. There was no argument. I wrapped her little body in my arms, held back my tears, and said, "Yes."

But after a few days I was needed back at the studio. During the summer, when Meg and I were in San Francisco on our cross-country trip, she had performed at the Full Moon Coffee House. This was a small venue that held around fifty women. We had decided that for the album, her song "Ode to a Gym Teacher" should be recorded in front of a live audience so that we could capture the exuberant laughter from the audience. Full Moon was chosen because it was close enough to Oregon so that Joan could drive down with her equipment and do the recording. All of that worked well. But when we listened in the studio, we realized the audience was too small, the response too tepid. We needed to find a way to fix it.

What we really needed was a new audience, one that hadn't heard the song before, and we weren't likely to find that in DC, where Meg had been performing "Gym Teacher" at every gig for months. And we didn't have time to book a concert someplace we hadn't been, get Meg and Joan and the equipment up there, and hope for the best. What else could we do? We decided to create a laugh track. I'm a good laugher, so I was called in.

There were probably ten of us in the studio—all the Olives (except Meg), friends we'd invited, Cris, and some of the musicians who played on the album, including Margie Adam. Joan played Meg's recording of the song over the speakers and miked us laughing and sighing and carrying on, as if we were there at the Full Moon. I had never noticed until this moment that some people laugh out—exhaling and making noise—and some people laugh in. They inhale when they laugh, and so it might as well be silent. Unfortunately, we had a couple of in-laughers. We ended up doubling and tripling the laugh track until we finally felt it sounded like a large and raucous audience.

Eventually, after burning through more hours and more dollars than I thought we could afford, we finished the recording. It was time to do the mix. Meg asked Margie to stick around and provide another set of ears. Judy had completed her six-month recording class and was helping and learning from Joan. Meg and Cris had gotten into a groove of silliness and they were constantly cracking each other up, in ways that nobody else understood or thought was funny. It didn't matter because they did. A lot of wine was drunk and a lot of dope was smoked. That also didn't matter, or else it did, but it seemed to help Meg, Cris, and Margie work well together and to like what they heard.

One night, I called Jennifer in Albuquerque. It was hard for me that she and Kate could not be a part of this, harder for them. So much was riding on this album. She and Kate were getting ready to give up their home, their good jobs, their community, to move to LA and throw in with this project that they had to take on faith far more than the rest of us. When we were almost finished, I called and told her. We were tired. We were over budget. We were behind schedule. But we were so happy with what was happening, with the music and the way everyone was working together. This was not a pipe dream. It was real.

There was much more to be done.

To shoot the album cover, we hired Joan Biren, one of the old Furies, who now called herself JEB. JEB had become serious about learning photography and documenting lesbian lives. We chose a photo that had Meg sitting on one of the stone pedestals in our backyard, looking very impish, with Nipper, son of Sappho, in the middle of the ivy that covered the small hill behind our house. We gathered all the players and the crew together for a group shot and used that on the back cover.

We would later catch a huge amount of flak from different groups of women—on the one hand, some said, Meg shouldn't be sitting down. This was too weak a position. On the other, said others, Meg shouldn't be on a pedestal. Were we implying that she should be worshiped? This pattern would repeat itself endlessly throughout my time at Olivia. One year, for example, at the Michigan Womyn's Music Festival, four different flyers were circulated about us. One accused us of being too separatist; one not separatist enough. One accused us of being capitalists and another of being socialists.

From Albuquerque, Kate designed the jacket and the album insert. Jennifer and I wrote the blurbs about Olivia and Meg. The Olivia blurb said, in part,

Our purposes are to make high quality women's music available to the public, to give women musicians access to the recording industry, to offer training in the technical, musical, and other fields related to the recording industry, and to provide jobs with decent pay in non-oppressive conditions. All money raised from record sales and contributions will be used for the purchase of our own studio, the production of future records, and the training and salaries of the women involved in Olivia. The owners of this company are the women who work for it.

Meg's blurb identified her as a "feminist singer, songwriter, guitarist and autoharpist." We were cautious about revealing too much of our politics and our revolutionary intentions. And although we left hints everywhere—including calling it *I Know You Know*, on this album, we never used the word "lesbian." We believed that if we could just get women to listen, if we could just reach their hearts, the rest wouldn't be so hard. But if we broadcast our lesbianism on the record, they wouldn't listen, and we wouldn't have a chance with them.

One day in early November, a package arrived at our house. Kate had sent a mock-up of the jacket. Oh my god—what a thrill. It was real. The record was real. We were real. And even though I had proofed the copy several times, Meg had managed to slip in a sweet little surprise. She and I had taken to calling each other "babycakes," which we shortened to BC's. She had added a line in the credits that said, "Thank you, BC's." I could not have been more touched and happy. The night the mock-up arrived, we took it to bed with us and slept with it. Seriously.

Shortly after, Meg and I had a party at our house. We invited scores of women, including some who had played on the album, our friends, women we hung out with at the bars, women we played softball with, Meg's guitar students—our house was jammed. We had a tape of the album and we wanted to play it for them. We wanted these women—our community—to be the first to hear *I Know You Know*. The response was stunning. A few days later, I wrote a letter to Cris to let her know what happened:

> They danced to everything, including "The Hive" and "Mama." They went berserk over the bees [buzzing sounds produced with synthesizer], and the strings, and the sax, and all the right things. They sang "Hello Hooray" at the top of their lungs. And they circle danced to "Joanna" [Cris's song]. Now I don't know if you know how heavy that is—the last time anybody circle danced around here was 3 years ago when a mass of women came out and went to the gay bars and were too afraid to touch each other and into putting down women who danced slow together as male-identified. But there was like this feeling of oh my god we have to be with everyone for this song, because it is such a song—I don't know what the word is—its [*sic*] been the theme song (or some kind of favorite) of this community for years—and to hear it on the record, with the fiddle (such as it is) and old CW herself singing the backup, and little MC having it on her album, was just too much for everybody. So I thought you'd like to know that.

But then the troubles began. Before there was digital, everything was analog. The eight tracks of music were mixed down to two tracks and sent off to a mastering lab from which a test acetate was created. Joan and Judy were handling this part of the process, Judy mostly following Joan's lead. There were problems with the acetate, and it took way too long to get a clean sound. The next step was to get and approve a test pressing from the

Meg and I had a party at our house in DC and played a test pressing of *I Know You Know* for our friends for the first time.

pressing plant in Los Angeles. We were using the plant that Joan used for her records, owned by Bud Waddell. Bud kept sending us test pressings, and we kept hearing sounds that were not supposed to be there. He would try again, and we would reject again.

We began to panic. We had done a fair amount of publicity for the album in the feminist press and at Meg's concerts, announcing the impending arrival of *I Know You Know*, encouraging advance orders and promising delivery in time for holiday gift-giving. The orders were pouring in. And we were still hearing a constant "whoosh" throughout the whole test pressing under the music. It was clear we weren't going to have albums to ship for the holidays.

Kate and Jennifer came up with the idea of a gift certificate that we would send out to everyone who had placed an order. Brilliant! Kate designed it so it fit in a regular business envelope. This gave us a temporary respite, but still left a lot of women disappointed and angry.

You will soon receive a copy of Olivia Records' first album, *Meg Christian: I know you know*. It is a gift from:

Meg Christian is a feminist singer, song-writer, guitarist and autoharpist. After graduating from the University of North Carolina with a degree in music, Meg came to Washington, DC and performed professionally in the city's nightclubs for five years. Two years ago she decided to concentrate exclusively on making music for women, and since then she has travelled all over the country singing women's music — music that speaks honestly and realistically to women about our lives: our needs, our strengths, our relationships with each other, our anger, our love. Olivia Records is a national women's recording company. Our purposes are to make high quality women's music available to the public, to give women musicians access to the recording industry, to offer training in the technical, musical and other fields related to the recording industry, and to provide jobs with decent pay in non-oppressive conditions. We are a non-profit corporation and have applied for tax-exempt status. All money raised from record sales and contributions will be used for the purchase of our own studio, the production of future records, and the training and salaries of the women involved in Olivia. The owners of this company are the women who work for it.
The album will be mailed to you as soon as we receive it from the presser. There is no need to send in this certificate.

Olivia Records · P.O. Box 1784 · Washington, DC 20013

The gift certificate that bought us more time

Try as we might, we could not get the pressing plant to hear what we were hearing, and what we were hearing was unacceptable. As winter approached, we spent our time arguing with the plant, sending out gift certificates and apologies, and starting to pack for our move to Los Angeles.

We sent Jennifer and Kate out to find us a place to live and they did—a three-bedroom house on Gramercy Drive in the Wilshire district. It had a big kitchen, a dining room that we would convert into the Olivia office, a small porch that would be Meg's music room, a tiny eating area, a living room, one bathroom, and a little playhouse in the back yard.

In DC, Meg, Judy, and I rented a truck and loaded everything we owned. Judy sold her car, so we had the big truck and the yellow station wagon. We put Elf, Nipper, and Evelyn in the back of the wagon and hit the road. The trip was not without its challenges—the cats were particularly unhappy about being in the car all day and in strange motel rooms at night. And the governor on our truck, which was supposed to keep us from going faster than 60 mph, was stuck somewhere around 50, which was fine when the highways were flat, but meant we could barely make it up some of the big hills—also known as mountains—that stood between DC and Los Angeles. We didn't know the governor was stuck. We just assumed that

The whole crew who made *I Know You Know*
Photo by JEB

trucks were slow. We ended up feeling like we had practically pushed the truck all the way from DC, but we finally arrived in LA in the middle of March, so happy to be there and so ready to get this album out.

Judy went immediately to the pressing plant and made them listen with her. "Oh," they said. "You mean that 'whish' sound. Sure, we can get rid of that." Already we were learning something important about the music industry. We had called it "whoosh." But, clearly, it was "whish." No wonder they didn't know what we were talking about.

We finally had records, and we started shipping them out. We were deliriously happy. And then we started getting complaints and returns. The record skipped. At first we thought people just had bad needles. But there were far too many complaints for this to be a problem of bad needles. And so we want back to the pressing plant and pressured them to re-press all 5,000 records. We recalled as many as we could and started shipping again.

And then, at last, LF 902 was out. Women had the first Olivia Records album, Meg's first album, the music we had waited so long for.

8 A CHORDING TO THE PEOPLE

Stories from the Road

BEFORE THE ADVENT OF DIGITAL music and the Internet, musicians made records and then went on tour in order to sell records. Record companies subsidized tours, and only a few—primarily the big stadium acts—made money. Radio stations were always anxious to get musicians on the air, and that often led to more airplay, which led to increased record sales. In the '80s and '90s there was a great deal more vertical integration, meaning that the radio station was owned by the same corporation that owned the concert promotion company that owned the best-placed billboards. Everything worked together to sell more records. The Internet completely upended that system. Sales of records plummeted. People who are actually still willing to pay for music are much more likely to download a song than an album. Now, musicians record and release music in order to support touring because that's where the money is.

In the early days of Olivia, touring was about selling records and much more. The money from Meg's gigs, however, supported all five of us in the collective, so of course we struggled over our need to generate money on the one hand and our desire to live without exploiting anyone on the other. We didn't know where the line was and were more inclined to undercharge than overcharge, which made us resentful when a woman would complain about a $1 ticket price while wearing an expensive Nikon camera around her neck.

When Meg performed at colleges, we got a small guarantee from the college so that most of the concerts were free to students. I kept track of the shows Meg did in late 1973 and early 1974 and the money we made.

Towson State College, Baltimore, MD	$75
St. Mary's College, St. Mary's City, MD	$150 + reimbursement for expenses
Hollins College, Roanoke, VA	$150 the first time, $200 the second
Montgomery College, Rockville, MD	$200
Cornell University, Ithaca, NY	$150 + reimbursement for expenses
Northrop High School, Ft. Wayne, IN	$200 + reimbursement for expenses
Johns Hopkins University, Baltimore, MD	$200
University of Connecticut, Storrs, CT	$250
Goddard College, Plainfield, VT	$300 + $50 reimbursement
Swarthmore College, Swarthmore, PA	$125
Bryn Mawr College, Bryn Mawr, PA	$100

The amounts seem paltry now, but at that time you could buy a new car for $3,000, a gallon of gas for 53¢, a dozen eggs for 78¢, and a record album for $6. The rent on our fully furnished, two-story, two-bedroom house in DC was $225 a month.

We also played at women's centers, lesbian bars, and women's coffee houses. With some exceptions, like The Saints bar in Boston, which seemed spacious and elegant by comparison, these were usually small and dark and, often, in the basement. But as long as there was a sound system—however rudimentary—we would go there. We either passed the hat or worked out a split from the ticket sales. Ticket prices were low, and, in addition, almost everyone used a sliding scale.

If we wanted to do a concert someplace where there was no bar or coffeehouse, I would find someone—maybe we had a distributor, or maybe there was a women's bookstore, or a newspaper or radio show, or even a woman on our mailing list—and ask her to produce a concert. I told them it wasn't too hard, that I had never done it before I did it, and now I was pretty good at it. The first question was, did they want to have a Meg Christian concert in their town? Were there other women who did too? Great. Get them together and follow these steps: Find a space and rent it; rent a simple sound system; being able to light the stage is a bonus (actually, having a stage is a bonus); make posters; sell tickets. The women who eventually formed the production collectives and companies, which ultimately became a nationwide network, were as fierce in their commitment to Women's Music and feminist values as we were. They operated without hierarchies; they prioritized working with women or women's businesses to supplement what they couldn't do themselves; they kept ticket prices reasonable; they offered free child care at the concerts; they did what they could to build community.

Most of the women who came to these early gigs were young and white. Probably many of them were lesbians, but coming out, especially in the colleges and small towns, was risky, so unless women were out as lesbians—and many were—we didn't know. Regardless, the response was almost always electric. Meg was an accomplished, skillful musician and a powerful performer who put together strong sets of music—both her own and songs by other women. The songs were not about pleasing men, or wanting men, or leaving men, or being left by men. In fact, the songs were not about men at all. This in itself was revolutionary. In contrast to most pop songs of the day, the songs celebrated women's strength and beauty, intelligence and daring. There were love songs to particular women and love songs to the community of women. Sometimes they were overtly feminist; sometimes they were funny, sometimes deeply moving. They validated women's experiences and put women at the center of their own lives. Meg was not the only musician doing this, so this upsurge of women musicians playing for mostly women audiences created a kind of energy that was reproducing itself and spreading all over the country, and, indeed, to other parts of the world.

Meg was funny and charming and warm and personable, and audiences loved her. The appreciation went beyond her music and her presentation. For a lot of women she represented the embodiment of all the new consciousness, all the changes we wanted to make and were making. That was, of course, an unfair burden to put on her, and so women were sometimes disappointed and angry when she showed herself to be a human being. But for the most part, they were thrilled to see her. Sometimes the response was a bit overwhelming. I remember a concert in Boston, in 1975, in a large hall that might have been on the campus of Boston University. Meg walked out onto the stage and was literally knocked backward by the waves of energy that the audience sent her way.

When Meg and I went on the road in the early and mid '70s, we would likely do a concert, recruit and/or meet with distributors, sit for interviews with the feminist press and the women's radio shows, go to a women's community potluck dinner, meet with the concert production collective immediately before and/or after the concert, and conduct a workshop the day after the concert. A lot of this work was pretty grueling for Meg, who, when she wasn't on stage, was really an introvert. But she was a trooper, and, more than that, she was determined to act like and be seen as a regular person who just had talents and skills that were different from, but not better or more valuable than, any other woman. So she joined in almost all the extra-concert activities, even if somewhat reluctantly at times.

I, on the other hand, was in heaven. What the right wing said about us was true—we *did* have an agenda and I *was* always recruiting. I got to talk endlessly with women about our vision and our values and I felt like I was Ginny Appleseed, spreading the gospel of lesbian feminism. I led workshops on how collectives work, how Olivia raised and spent our money and how we thought about money, the importance of women-only spaces, what it meant to start a feminist business, how to understand class, and how to include more women of color in the women's movement. On our tours, we were not just selling records and we were not just promoting Meg. We were selling Olivia, not as a brand, but as a set of politics. And we were building community.

Women wanted to be connected—not necessarily to Olivia—but to some piece of this fast-growing movement. Some approached Meg with songs they thought she might include in her repertoire, and sometimes she did. Some came to workshops to find out how to start a concert production company, and we ended up working with many of them. Others came to find women in their community who were also on fire about feminism and lesbianism and making big changes.

Of course, some came to argue, to criticize, and to demand that we change something that they didn't like. There were those, like the Seattle Separatists, who thought we weren't political enough; there were those who thought we should not perform anywhere if the space could not be women-only; there were those who thought we should encourage men to come to concerts. Later, there were those who were furious at us for working with Sandy Stone, who is transgender. We listened, we argued back; sometimes we learned something.

We almost always stayed in women's homes, and usually we had a bed with clean sheets and food in the refrigerator. But not always. There were times when we were presented with a couch covered in dog hair for one of us and a sleeping bag on the floor for the other. We might be left alone in a city we knew nothing about, with no car, and with half a container of expired sour cream as provisions. Sometimes the women were careful of our need for a tiny bit of privacy, other times, not so much.

Once, we were in a college town, staying in the home of the concert producer whom we shall call Suzanne Weldon, not her real name. We hadn't met Suzanne before. She had contacted us about producing a Meg concert, she was a lesbian, and she seemed to know something about production. What else did we need? Suzanne, however, was a hoverer. Wherever we were in the house, she was right behind us. When we got into bed for the night, she stood in the doorway and stared at us. We finally had to ask her to close the door and let us get some sleep. When we woke up in the morning she was standing just outside the bedroom door waiting for us. We couldn't wait to get out of there.

Fast forward twelve years to 1986. My partner Raye and I were having Thanksgiving dinner with friends at our house in Oakland, and one of our friends asked if she could bring a friend who was visiting from out of town and who called herself Heartful. "Of course," we said. Most of the women at the table were then or had been involved in Women's Music. We were having a great old time, laughing a lot, eating delicious food, and we started telling stories about life on the road in the '70s, and in particular, horror stories. I proceeded to talk about this horrible woman, the hoverer, how she had creeped us out, and everyone was gasping appropriately at the details, and I asked,

"Did any of you ever work with her? Her name is Suzanne Weldon." Now there was a different kind of gasping going on. And then the woman who called herself Heartful said, "I am Suzanne Weldon." Oh. Thank god we both still smoked. In what might be one of the smoothest moves I've ever made in my life, I said to her, "Let's go outside and have a cigarette." We did. She told me she had been pretty drunk the whole time Meg and I were there, and she felt terrible about the experience and was profoundly apologetic. I easily accepted her apology, apologized to her for making fun of her, and we went back into the house and finished dinner and told more stories and everyone could see that Heartful and I had worked it out and we just had a good time.

There was one memorable occasion when we did stay at a hotel. Meg was invited to perform at the National NOW (National Organization for Women) Conference in Philadelphia in October 1975. This both was and was not a big deal. On the one hand, this concert would expose Meg and Olivia to women who probably didn't know much about us but could become important contacts for future concerts and record sales. On the other hand, we believed that NOW was a reformist organization whose overarching goal was equality with men. We were a bit dismissive of them; we thought their aspirations uninspired and weak, and their programs were puny. Nevertheless, being asked to be the main entertainment at the National NOW Conference meant that somebody on the conference organizing committee was aware of Women's Music and Meg Christian, and that was a good thing. And so we went. The conference was held at the Bellevue-Stratford Hotel (which became famous a year later as ground zero for the first outbreak of Legionnaires' cisease). The concert was supposed to begin at eight o'clock, after the election of officers and board members. NOW was going to open the concert to the public, and our Philadelphia distributor had done a lot of publicity to make sure that the larger lesbian and feminist communities would show up.

But the election of officers did not go according to plan. (In fact, we learned later that it was one of the most bitterly contested elections NOW ever had.) Meg and I were told that we would be called from our hotel room when they were ready for us, and so we waited. And waited. About once an hour someone would call up to our room and let us know how much longer they thought it would be, and they were always wrong. Meanwhile, we heard from our distributor that there was a line of several hundred women outside the hotel waiting to get in for the concert. This was Meg's first concert in Philadelphia, and women were excited to hear her and be part of this large gathering of feminists. And so they waited and waited. Meg was playing her guitar. I was distractedly watching TV.

At around eleven o'clock, we decided we needed to do something. It was becoming clear to us that this concert was not going to happen. Meg put her guitar down and said, "I feel terrible about all these women waiting outside for hours."

"I know. It's too bad there are so many of them, or we could have them up to our room and do a concert here."

And then we both got it. I jumped up and said, "Let's go out on the street, to the line where they're waiting. Maybe you can do a couple of songs."

Meg put her guitar in its case, wrapped a scarf around her neck to protect her throat, and we went down into the street. We asked the women at the front of the line to let the women behind them know that Meg was going to sing for them right here and now, and they should come in close because there was no sound system. I explained what was happening inside, that we doubted if the concert was ever going to happen, and that this was the best we could do. And so a hundred or more women—all that were left from the four-hour wait—gathered around, and, for twenty minutes or so, Meg gave them a piece of the concert they had come for. She ended with "Ode to a Gym Teacher," and everyone sang along. This was a moment of grace. Our dreams for Olivia, our vision for the world we wanted, our capacities to rise to any occasion, and the love we felt for and from the women in the street—everything seemed perfectly aligned.

The NOW meeting finally adjourned at two in the morning. We were sound asleep.

There were other moments. Meg and I arrived in Toronto in a blizzard. The concert was in a church. Meg was in the middle of her first set, and all the power went out. There were two huge candelabras on the sides of the stage, and some women rushed forward in the dark, moved the candelabras to the center, lit the candles, and voila! The audience could once again see Meg, and Meg could see her guitar. But of course there was no amplification, so all two hundred women moved up into the first few rows and squeezed in so Meg didn't have to shout. These women would not be denied their Women's Music concert.

In Pittsburgh, the concert was at the YMCA, and the women's community was legally blocked from holding it as women-only space. The room was packed with close to two hundred women and maybe two men. I was sitting behind the mixing board watching the crowd, and I noticed one of the concert organizers standing in the back of the room crying. I approached her cautiously, with no idea what could be wrong, but a lot of anxiety. She tried to stanch the flow of tears, but instead she started sobbing. "Look at this," she blubbered. "This is my community. This is the first time I've seen us all together. I'm so happy I could cry. Oh," and then she started to laugh, "I guess I am crying."

Salt Lake City. We had amused ourselves for hours with stories about Mormons and lesbians. Will they run us out of town? Will we inspire a rebellion and run them out of town? Will we turn into pillars of salt? We were actually a little nervous about the concert—will anybody come other than the three women who are producing it? In a rare moment of extravagance, we decided to go out to dinner. We chose a restaurant on the main drag and we were shocked to see that every single person eating dinner was a woman. Had we stumbled upon Salt Lake City's secret lesbian gathering place? The women didn't really look like lesbians—they were all wearing dresses and seemed a bit frumpy...but still. Maybe this was what they had to do to survive under the watchful gaze of the Mormon Church. Alas, we learned when we met up with our hosts that this was not a secret lesbian restaurant. There was a big church meeting that night, and only men were allowed to attend, so lots of wives took themselves out to dinner. They didn't show up at the concert, but over one hundred brave feminists and lesbians did. Meg and I left Salt Lake the next day and did not look back...just in case.

9 IF IT WEREN'T FOR THE MUSIC

**Building the Distribution Network and
Expanding the Revolutionary Web**

GETTING OUR RECORDS INTO WOMEN'S hands was not the
glamorous part of Olivia, but it was an essential piece, and,
as with everything else we did, we made up our own way to
do it. It was creative, politically astute, visionary, and doomed
to failure.

In the heyday of the music business, when LPs (for long
playing at 33 rpm) were made of vinyl and jackets were twelve-
inch squares, there were record stores in every city and town in
the country. There were chains like Tower Records, Sam Goody,
Wherehouse, Rainbow Records, Waxie Maxie, and Licorice
Pizza, and there were thousands of independent stores like
Leopold's in Berkeley, Other Music in Manhattan, Electric
Fetus in Minneapolis, and Waterloo Records in Austin. The
big chains usually bought their records directly from the labels.
The indies bought from one-stops, which were basically large
warehouses that bought records on consignment from the major
and independent labels and re-sold them to the record stores. It
was not unheard of, but pretty rare, for an independent record
company to bypass the one-stops and go directly to the chains
and indies, yet that is what we did.

I believed, for several reasons, that having our own distribution network was crucial to the vision of Olivia. First, I thought

that having a distributor in every city and town—a woman who felt strongly connected to Women's Music and the goals of Olivia—meant having a revolutionary cadre in every town, and we would have a nationwide network of women using music to organize their communities around feminist and lesbian feminist issues and politics. Second, every record that was sold by a distributor put money in her pocket, which we hoped would lead to economic independence for at least some. And finally, we wanted to be represented by people who shared our passions and our politics, and that had to be women. After our catalog grew, and it was clear that some of our records were selling well (for an independent label), we were occasionally approached by one-stops who wanted to carry our records, but we always turned them down.

This model really represents what turned out to be the ultimate contradiction of Olivia Records: how to be a revolutionary political organization and a sustainable business at the same time. Even when the distributors sold other products—other Women's Music labels, as well as books and other feminist goodies—they couldn't sell enough in their tiny territories, and we wanted tiny territories because we saw the distributors as organizers. At one point we had separate distributors for Berkeley, Oakland, and San Francisco. So what was it going to be? A way for women to make a righteous living or a way for women to get deep into the politics of one geographic community and become catalysts for change?

But we didn't see these contradictions at the time. We believed we could do it all. At every concert where Meg performed, I gave a short rap about the vision of Olivia, urged people to buy records (which were always on sale in the lobby—either by the local women's bookstores or a woman who volunteered—and, later, by the local distributor), and asked any women who were interested in becoming distributors to meet me in the lobby after the concert. There were always a few women who came to see me. I would explain how it worked: we sent them the records on consignment, they did their best to sell everywhere—women's and leftist bookstores, listening parties at their homes to which they would invite women from the community, and, yes, mainstream, male-owned, patriarchal, capitalistic record stores and the even more evil chains. Some of them would drift away at that point. I would then tell those who were still listening about the money—they had to collect from all the stores they sold to, and every month they had to send in a report of what they had sold and to whom, along with a check for everything they had collected. And then we would send them a commission check for 15% of what they sold. After a certain amount of time, they would have to return to us any records they had in stock that hadn't been sold. This turned out to be way too complicated and unworkable. For one thing, mainstream record stores were buying from distributors on consignment—this is how the business worked. So a distributor might "sell" ten copies of *I Know You Know* to a local store, but the store would pay monthly for what it had sold, which might be three records. At one point, we had over one hundred distributors, and the bookkeeping on our end became nightmarish. Plus, we were regularly writing commission checks for $20 or less. One of our constant refrains was "nobody will get rich at Olivia Records," but this was ridiculous.

In these early days, women didn't want to get involved for the possible financial benefits. They were moved by the music or the vision or the longing to be connected to our very powerful idea. I would explain how it worked and then ask them each to tell me why they were interested. (What an excellent way to conduct a job interview—in the lobby of a concert hall or in a bar, coffee house, or club, surrounded by dozens or hundreds of women buzzing after a concert, with your potential competitors listening in on your descriptions!) And then I would pick someone. Sometimes it was actually easy. After a concert in LA, two women stepped up to be distributors. One told me that she knew Bob Dylan and could use her connection to get us into record stores. The other said she worked at Sisterhood Books and had some ideas about how to get better placement for the records in the women's bookstores. That was Robin Brooks, who became our first LA distributor and eventually joined the collective, working with me on expanding and managing the growing distribution network.

Over the eight years I was with Olivia, the distribution network grew and went through numerous changes. We lost a lot of records and money to distributors who just disappeared. We started working with women who wanted to make a successful business selling Olivia and other women's records and also producing concerts. They wanted more territory to cover, and they were serious about selling to the chains, so we began moving in the direction of fewer, more economically sustainable distributors. We got rid of the commission system and had the distributors buy records from us outright (always on consignment) and keep whatever markup they could get. We sometimes organized distributors' meetings at the Women's Music festivals that were becoming part of the landscape of the '70s; sometimes at these meetings we would organize ourselves by region. These were wonderful opportunities for me to see women I had met once for five minutes. When we had the money, Robin would also come. These meetings gave the distributors a sense of community with each other. They gave us all an opportunity to talk about how women were dealing with certain problems: Who had had success with which chain, and how did they do it? Did anyone know how to…? And they gave us important feedback on how the distribution system

A meeting of the Olivia distributors in Austin

was operating from their perspective and what women in their communities were saying about the music.

I remember these meetings as being particularly fruitful and fun. I was on my way to one such meeting with a cassette tape of the soon-to-be-released album by the San Francisco Bay Area band BeBe K'Roche. I was very excited about giving them a first listen. This was our third album, and it did what we wanted—broke the mold of the singer-songwriter as the only expression of Women's Music. In those days, the airport security system was thought to destroy film and tape, and so I handed the cassette to the security person, walked through the security machine, got on the plane and realized when we were at thirty thousand feet that I had left the tape at the airport. We were all so disappointed. The distributors insisted that I sing the album for them. What a really terrible idea that was! I have the vocal range of a small frog and had a very hard time staying on key. And BeBe K'Roche was a rock band. How was I going to sing all of *that*? But we had a wonderful rapport, and so I did what I could and they thought they would love the album when they actually got to hear it.

Fairly early on, we were approached by other women artists who had recorded on their own labels, and we thought this was a good way for us to support these other artists, have more product for our distributors to sell, and make a little money for Olivia. We had Kay Gardner's *Mooncircles,* albums by the Berkeley Women's Music Collective, and even a 45 rpm by Bobi Jackson and her jazz-blues group High Risk.

The distribution network ultimately morphed into a much smaller set of independent, women-owned companies like Ladyslipper in North Carolina, Goldenrod in Michigan, Zango covering everything from Northern California through Oregon and Washington, and a few others. These women carried full catalogs of Women's Music, as well as records on other independent labels. The distribution network was one of our great and lasting contributions to the women's movement in general, but it was also a source of contentiousness and in-fighting in the world of Women's Music.

The problems began for us in late 1975 when Margie Adam decided she did not want to wait for Olivia to record her, and she formed her own label—Pleiades Records—with her lover and business partner Barbara (Boo) Price (the same Boo Price whom I had met in college). Margie's album was released in 1976 and was distributed, in most cities, by the women we thought of as Olivia distributors. Boo had approached many of them directly and asked them to distribute Margie's album.

We only found out what they were doing when some of the distributors came to us because they felt conflicted. Olivia had trained them (to the extent that they had been trained) and had basically set them up in business. They asked us if it would be okay with us if they took on Margie's album as well as the Olivia catalog. Some distributors had already agreed to take it on, and legally, the distributors were free to do what they wanted. It would only help them economically if they had more records to sell, especially one by Margie that was bound to sell well. But in one instance, Boo bypassed one of our best distributors, Betsy York, who was selling up a storm in Boston, and instead recruited her former college roommate. Sidestepping Betsy in Boston made no sense, and signaled to me that Boo and Margie were probably not interested in building a network or an alternative economy, that their first priority was promoting Margie.

In any case, we felt ripped off. Neither Boo nor Margie had discussed this with us. They just did it. It felt like they were taking advantage of the work that we had done without even acknowledging us in the process. They had a way of making decisions that was completely contrary to the principles by which we were trying to live. The disagreement was typical of the issues that would surface again over the years and would remain among the tensions between us.

But, in the spring of 1975, we were focused on something else.

10 BRAND NEW THING
Sharing the Load

THE FIVE OLIVES SAT IN a circle on the floor in the kitchen of our new home in LA. It was spring 1975. The three cats and Jennifer's Old English Sheepdog Moxie wandered in and out. I was exhausted and very stressed out.

"I am carrying too much. This whole company is in my head and it is making me crazy. Everyone has little pieces but I am carrying way too much. I need help."

This was a rare admission for me. I wanted to feel like I could do anything and everything, but I was having too much trouble holding it all. We assumed our next album would be Cris's, but that was now complicated by her involvement with Margie. They had become lovers during the making of *I Know You Know* (*IKYK*) (this was a year before Margie and Boo Price became lovers), and now they were proposing a double album with one record for each woman and a number of duets throughout. Cris was the obvious next step for us, but Margie was not. We didn't think we could afford to produce two albums at once, but, more than that, we were unwilling to feature white women singer-songwriters on our first three albums. That would define Women's Music in a way that was too limiting. Our musical/political vision was much bigger than that, and we wanted to make that statement by producing a different kind of music as soon as we could. Cris and I were writing letters to each other, trying to find our footing, trying to solidify our relationship or define it in a way that worked for Cris and for Olivia. The high of producing *IKYK* was over, and it seemed we had landed back on earth with a thud.

Right after we arrived in LA, we were approached by some women representing the Los Angeles Women's Building. This was a huge edifice in downtown that was the first of its kind in the country. Primarily intended as a space for women artists, it had galleries and studios, and it also had space for concerts and dances. The women who approached us were producing a benefit for the building, to be called Building Women. They had already lined up Cris, Margie, The New Miss Alice Stone Ladies Society Orchestra, Holly Near, and Lily Tomlin. They wanted Meg to join them and they wanted me to stage-manage. The concert would be in June at the Wilshire Ebell Theater, an intimate and grand old theater which had staged performances by Judy Garland, Dave Brubeck, Tito Puente, the Blind Boys of Alabama, and hundreds of other musicians, comics and performing artists. Of course we said yes. This meant a lot of time would be spent by both Meg and me in rehearsals.

I was also running the distribution network, which was growing by leaps and bounds and wrestling with the contradictions of a great political and terrible business idea. Women all over the country wanted to connect with what we were doing, and we were happy to have them. So I was constantly dealing with "training" new distributors, shipping out records, collecting money from their sales, figuring their commissions and sending them out, trying to stay on top of the women who got records to sell and then didn't send in reports or money, settling disputes about territory, trying to convince those who were reluctant to sell records outside of women's bookstores, trying to figure out how to get into the big chains, keeping track of sales.

Along with Meg, I was the public face of Olivia. I did the press and radio interviews, I spoke at all her concerts, I represented Olivia on various panels, I wrote most of the copy that we used for publicity and for promoting our ideas. I also was in conversation with several musicians who had produced their own albums and wanted Olivia to distribute them. And I was carrying on a regular correspondence and negotiations with Cris and Margie. There were no quick emails. There were long letters, typed or handwritten and sent through the US mail. I would say things in my letters to them that could be taken one way or another, that could make relations better or worse, and I would have to wait days or weeks to get a response. I was stressed out and I needed help.

Jennifer was the first to speak up. "I would like to take over all the business aspects. I'll keep the books, write the checks, do the budgeting. I'd also like to write more."

Great. I totally trusted Jennifer and I knew she would come through.

Kate saw herself as a designer and didn't feel she had the skills to do much more. But she said she really enjoyed doing mindless repetitive tasks and she was willing to help out in whatever way she could: packing and shipping records, keeping on top of our growing mailing list, writing thank you notes for donations, etc.

There wasn't more Meg could take on. She was performing a lot, writing more, and doing interviews. She was also listening to the dozens of tapes that came in every month from women who either wanted to record for Olivia or wanted Meg to record or perform one of their songs. She listened and responded to all of them. Plus, she and Kate were now working on a songbook of *IKYK* that we wanted to publish.

That left Judy. "I want more power." Judy had volunteered to be president of the company when we incorporated (we had tried to get nonprofit status, but the IRS decided we were a business and not an educational institution). I had thought that was a little bold of her under the circumstances, but I also thought it didn't matter. The titles were for the government. They would have no impact on how we worked. Now, here was Judy saying she wanted more power.

An uncomfortable silence ensued. And then I said, "You don't know enough to have more power. You need to learn more. You need to get involved beyond the technical aspects. Then you can have more power." I didn't have much room for kindness in those days. But Judy took it well and proceeded to get more involved in every aspect of Olivia. In fact, she was the last of the five of us to stay involved, and ultimately saved Olivia by getting it out of the music business before it imploded.

Jennifer asked me what parts I wanted to keep. "I want to keep working with the distributors and building that network. I want to keep writing and speaking and doing media, although I am happy to work with you. And, of course, I want to keep booking Meg, traveling with her, and building the concert production network. I want to be involved in every decision we make, but I really need everyone to know all the details that I have in my head so that we can make the decisions together."

After that meeting on the kitchen floor, we started to act and work more like a collective. Everybody really stepped up, and I was able to let go of a lot. We talked constantly about what we were doing and thinking and we were able to make big and small decisions with a unity of purpose and direction. I had never been in a collective that functioned so smoothly.

We were also learning to live collectively. Since we were living together, we decided to pool all our income. Judy and I were collecting unemployment. Meg was bringing in money from her concerts. Kate had been hired as the designer of *The New Woman's Survival Catalogue* and was actually spending a lot of time in New York. With just one album out, Olivia was demanding our full attention, and we wanted to give it. That meant living as close to the bone as we could, sharing as much as we could—our only car was the old, yellow Toyota wagon—and drawing as little as possible from the money coming into Olivia. We were compatible enough and our backgrounds were similar enough that we did this without a lot of tension or disagreement.

Meanwhile, tensions with Cris and Margie were mounting, and we were growing more frustrated and afraid about our next project. Cris was having doubts about her place in Olivia. In a letter she wrote to Meg and me she said,

> [I think we have] fears that we may not be able to work together due to our different dreams. Whenever this fear begins to flood my soul, I have to remember what it is that we have in common, what it is that I truly love about you two, in particular, and of course, there is the music…lest we forget. I guess that I am concerned about whether or not your dream includes my dream and vice versa…. I realize that as your dream stands, I am not the most logical representative. But I also know that it would mean a great deal if I choose to record for Olivia….
>
> [Olivia] matters to me as you do, and I am terribly frustrated in our relationship. I can't stand being uncomfortable, being under scrutiny, can't bear feeling guilty because my politics are not quite Olivia-accepted…above all, I hate being separated from you, my musical friend, Meg, you who make me swoon in all the right ways; and you, Ginny, my first teacher in

political awareness....I miss being your trusted, strong friend with all the privileges that position entails....

[T]he politics involved in the process have, in my mind, come to overshadow that which is at the <u>real</u> center, indeed the very heart of this process which is <u>music</u>, and the beautiful magical part of it....The final thing I wish to touch upon is that just as you doubt my total commitment to women, so I must say do I doubt your total commitment to <u>all</u> women. I do believe that some of the limits you choose to impose are not my limits. I have others.

Cris was not off the mark. She was passionate about the earth and water, and, when she spoke from the stage, these were the issues she spoke about. She rarely spoke directly about feminism, never about lesbianism, rarely about anything we considered "political." We wanted her to be more personable on stage, more woman-centered in her remarks, more accessible to the audiences in the ways that Meg was. We didn't like the way she wore her hair long and was always flipping it back like a straight woman. We worried that she would fly away. She worried that we would hold her down. When we finally learned to relax into each other, Cris, the Aquarius, called Meg, a Capricorn, and me, a Taurus, her earth shoes.

We later learned—from Margie herself—that Margie had been encouraging Cris's doubts and questions. She was insisting that Olivia was much too political for Cris and would soon enough cramp her musical expression. But Cris and Meg and I kept talking. We never stopped. We wanted each other to be different, but, through all that, we could never imagine the dream without each other. Eventually, we became easy with each other, but getting there took its own sweet time.

Once we decided not to pursue the double album, we wrote to both of them, and there followed a long silence. I finally called Cris. I couldn't have been more nervous.

"Cris," I said softly, "we have always assumed that the next Olivia album would be yours. So what happened? How did everything get so screwed up?"

"Well," she said, "you assumed. But you never asked me."

I thought about that. Was what she was saying true? Even possible? Well then, the next step was obvious.

"Cris, would you make our next album?"

"Yes," she said softly, almost whispering. Then a little louder. "Yes." And, finally, she thundered, "Yes, I will!"

Our whole history was a perfect example of a push-pull relationship. I would learn that for Cris everything was that easy, and that hard. We just kept trying, and we kept moving forward. And moving forward meant starting to plan for Cris's first Olivia album, which we would record in the summer of 1975.

11 SHOOTING STAR

Making *The Changer* and the Changed

CRIS WILLIAMSON WAS BORN IN South Dakota and grew up in the mountains of Colorado and Wyoming. Her father had been a forest ranger, and she grew up in the woods with few playmates but a huge imagination and a love for open spaces. She had made it abundantly clear that she hated boxes. And though we'd worked through so much together, the lenses through which we saw the world were still very different. Jump ahead for a moment to 1979. We were in the studio making Cris's second Olivia album—"Strange Paradise." I had been on the road with Meg, and, when I got back, Judy immediately pulled me aside.

"We're halfway through recording, and Cris won't sign the contract. We have already spent a small fortune on this record and we can't afford to stop. But we can't go on until we get an agreement with her."

For the first few Olivia albums, I had written all the contracts. I knew absolutely nothing about contracts or contract law, but I believed that our written agreements with each other should reflect our feminist values. These contracts were short and without many demands and probably completely unenforceable, but we never had to find out. Now, we were growing and had hired Boo Price to be our lawyer and write our contracts. I was shocked when I read Boo's first draft. It was pages long and protected us from dozens of possibilities and contingencies that I hadn't even known existed. This was close to the version of the contract Judy had been trying to get Cris to sign.

I went to the studio and asked Cris to talk to me.

"So, what's the problem with the contract?" I asked her.

"Look, I am a table and you are a chair." She really said this. "We have different roles, but we work together. We fit together. This contract makes it sound like we're enemies about to rip each other off. It does not have the energy of how I want our relationship to be."

"You are a table and Olivia is a chair?" I often felt like Cris and I came from different planets.

"Do you trust me? Do you really think I might steal the master tapes and give them to another company?"

"Okay," I said, understanding on a deeper level than ever before that Cris was not going to fly away. "I get it. So let me rewrite this. I think there are really three points we need to formally agree on. We own the master and the performances on the record. You own the songs you wrote and will get all the songwriting royalties. And you will get royalties on every record we sell. Is that it?"

She stuck out her hand to shake and then pulled me in for a hug. "Write it up and I'll sign it. Now I'm going to go make some beautiful music."

And she did.

But before there was *Strange Paradise*, there was *The Changer and the Changed*.

We went into the studio in the summer of 1975. By now the Olives were well-ensconced in our Los Angeles home. When we began recording, Cris and Margie were lovers, and, in the middle of the album, Margie broke up with Cris and began her relationship with Boo Price. I was beside myself. I had introduced

them to each other, and now I was sorry I had. Cris, needless
to say, was devastated. (There are some who've suggested that
some of the power of *The Changer and the Changed* came from
the very changes that Cris was going through.) But, while Cris
and Margie were in the studio together, they tried to get along.

Cris decided to move into the little playhouse in our back
yard for the duration of the album. Really, she just slept there
and occasionally played her guitar and did some yoga. We kept
our back door open so she could come in and out and use the
kitchen and bathroom. And during this time, Moxie, Jennifer's
Old English Sheepdog, fell utterly and completely in love with
Cris. Moxie wanted to move into the playhouse, but it wasn't
big enough for both of them. Whenever Cris would stroll into
our house, Moxie would immediately fall on her back with her
legs in the air and start whimpering. She could only be soothed
when Cris rubbed her belly.

Heartbreak aside, we had an album to make and a budget to
keep to. Joan Lowe came down from Oregon to engineer, and
Judy was by her side. Cris wanted to produce her own album,
and she counted heavily on the ears and advice of Meg, Margie,
and Marcy Dicterow, a professional string player, writer, and
arranger. As with all Olivia albums, Cris chose the musicians
she wanted to work with. The music scene in LA was much
more vibrant than DC, so she was able to draw on some artists
with significant recording experience, like Marcy Dicterow, who
arranged and conducted all the strings. June Millington—who,
in 1969, with her sister Jean, co-founded Fanny, one of the first
all-women rock bands—played electric and slide guitar. Jackie
Robbins played electric bass on every song but two, and on
those she played cello, adding a richness to the music. Meg put
down beautiful classical guitar parts and joined Vicki Randle
for supporting vocals. When Cris wasn't accompanying herself
on piano, Margie was. Cris had sent them all tapes and charts

of the songs and asked them to come in with their parts ready, and, for the most, part they did. Sometimes what they came in with was great; sometimes it needed tweaking. Sometimes Cris just didn't like her original idea for what it should sound like, and she and the musician and the "ears" would work out a new part.

I did not go to the studio every day. Judy was there, keeping an eye on the clock, and I worked most days in the office with Jennifer, filling orders, doing interviews, trying to get reviews, booking concerts, taking care of business.

One night in the middle of making the album, Cris went out to dinner with an old friend, and so we ended up with just the five of us at dinner. Jennifer made a batch of chiles rellenos, one of our favorite meals. We began eating in the silence of the hungry. After we had all had a few bites and were feeling less frantic, Kate turned to Judy and Meg and asked them how the day's recording went. Judy and Meg exchanged somewhat furtive glances, and I began to wonder what had gone on.

Judy took a sip of water. "We started laying down the backup vocals on 'Shooting Star.' Vicki and Meg really sounded good together."

Kate took another chile and said, "I thought today you were going to add some of the string parts."

Again, Judy and Meg eyed each other. Finally, Meg blurted out, "We tried, lord knows we tried."

Everyone now turned to Judy. She put down her fork. "I think we have a problem with Joan. She just...I don't know. I don't know if she can do stuff that's as complicated as this. Remember the problems we had with Meg's album, and that was only eight tracks."

"I thought that was all about the funky studio we were using," I said.

"Yeah," Judy answered, her face looking more grim by the minute. "But maybe not. Maybe it was her. Because there's nothing funky about the studio we're in now, and we're using sixteen tracks, and Joan is having a much harder time. Marcy and the other string players laid down a beautiful track, and Joan lost it."

Now we all stopped eating and looked at each other. This was serious, not only because we were wasting precious dollars in useless studio time, but also because we wanted quality. We needed an album that was technically as excellent as the music. And if Joan couldn't cut it, where would we ever find another woman engineer who could? Another woman engineer who loved what we were doing and was willing to work for the peanuts we paid? And how would we even approach Joan about this? We loved her; she was the one who had helped us navigate through so much in the early days.

Meg took a sip of wine. "I think Cris is starting to get a little frustrated."

Kate asked Judy, "How serious is this?"

"I'm not sure yet. It's not the first time she's screwed up, but I keep hoping she can fix it. You know we always say 'we'll fix it in the mix.' But you can't fix what you can't find. I think I'm trying to believe it will be okay, but more and more I'm worried."

Eventually, the string parts had to be recorded again, and, for the moment, there was nothing to be done but to keep on. But we were paying attention.

The last song Cris recorded was "Song of the Soul," a song that she closed most of her concerts with for decades. It became one of the hugely popular songs on the album, a great sing-along that probably came closest to expressing Cris's outlook on life.

> Open mine eyes that I may see
> Glimpses of truth thou hast for me
> Open mine eyes, illumine me
> Spirit divine.

"Love of my life," I am crying, I am not dying
I am dancing.
Dancing along in the madness, there is no sadness,
Only a song of the soul.

....

Come to your life like a warrior, nothin' will bore yer,
You can be happy
Let in the light it will heal you, and you can feel you
And sing out a song of the soul.

We invited dozens of women and girls to sing the chorus on the recording, Cris conducted us, and we had a great old time singing our hearts out.

By the time we finished, we still didn't know what to call the album, and finally a friend suggested a line from Cris's iconic song "Waterfall," the first song on the album.

Sometimes it takes a rainy day
Just to let you know
Everything's gonna be all right....
When you open up your life to the living, all things
come spilling in on you.
And you're flowing like a river, the Changer and
the Changed.
You got to spill some over, spill some over, spill some
over, over all.

It was a perfect description of who we were, who she was, what we were doing. The album—which is the best-selling album in Women's Music and may hold the record for healing more hearts and bringing more women out of the closet than any other—was called *The Changer and the Changed*. LF 904 was in the can.

12 Gimme Just a Little Bit More

Women on Wheels Rocks Us All

FTER THE SUCCESS OF THE Building Women Benefit for the
Los Angeles Women's Building, Marianne Schneller, an LA
peace activist, theatrical producer, and lesbian, decided that
this music, these musicians, needed to be presented properly—
"on proscenium stages, with real sound and lighting," she said,
"and it needed to be done NOW." Marianne had just completed
working with Holly Near, who was almost constantly touring
in support of the anti-Vietnam War movement and as part of
the Free the Army tour, which encouraged young men to resist
the draft and already-drafted soldiers to resist their orders. In
September of 1975, Marianne called a meeting at Holly's house
of the four soloists from Building Women—Meg, Cris, Margie,
and Holly—and asked them if they would participate in a tour.
Her idea was to hit as many cities as possible in California in
a two-week period in February 1976. The musicians agreed
and left Marianne to it. Nobody really had any idea what this
would entail, or what the impact would be. It just seemed like
a good idea, and here was someone who was willing to do it.

The tour was called Women on Wheels. It was a huge
success on many levels. It was a huge mess on many others.
And it was a personal disaster for me. It encapsulated so much

about what we were doing that was great and often beautiful, and so much that was challenging and sometimes ugly.

Between February 1 and February 15, 1976, there were eight concerts: San Diego, Santa Cruz, Sebastopol, Los Angeles, Santa Barbara, two in Oakland, and the California Institution for Women (CIW)—a state prison in Corona, sixty miles east of LA. Karlene Faith, who had been active for several years in the Santa Cruz Women's Prison Project, was the force behind the decision to bring the concert to CIW. Karlene was a close friend of Cris, and, in fact, had already brought Cris and Holly, as well as hundreds of other "outsiders," into the prison as part of an ongoing educational, political, and cultural program. Karlene's interest was in using the WOW tour to bring attention to imprisoned women because, as she said, "we see that imprisoned women sit at the junction of our failures to effectively combat an unjust social system." Karlene participated in the WOW planning meetings where we decided that instead of making speeches about women and the "justice" system from the stage, we would conduct a workshop in each city on the day after that city's concert. Karlene coordinated the workshops, which included discussion and a showing of *We're Alive*, a film produced by prisoners inside CIW with members of the Women's Film Workshop of UCLA.

With the exception of the CIW performance, every show sold out halls of one to two thousand people. "Women drove from four or five hours away," as Marianne said, "to come to a space and experience something they had never experienced before. Women would come in from these small towns—and maybe for the first time they were sitting among something that was familiar to them. That's what it was all about."

The "something" that many concert attendees had never experienced before was community, a sense of belonging, of finally knowing they were not "the only one"—whether they called themselves "lesbian" or "woman-identified" or "feminist" or they just had an inkling that how they were supposed to feel and look and be bore little or no relation to who they actually were. Women in cities and towns all over the country were having this experience, and it often happened around a concert of Women's Music, regardless of the performer. Women on Wheels put the four biggest draws in Women's Music at that time on stage together. The rooms were electric; the excitement was palpable; the response was generally ecstatic.

This was as true at CIW as at every other concert, where the two hundred or so women who were allowed to attend—plus the guards—hooted and hollered and laughed and cried. They raucously and tearfully shared their joy and gratitude. The musicians were not allowed to have any contact with the prisoners, so they just came in, set up, and did the show.

Every concert opened with "Hello Hooray," with Meg singing lead and playing guitar, Margie on piano, Cris and Holly on supporting vocals. After that, the order changed for each concert. Each woman did a solo set, and they also played in various combinations with each other. They always concluded with Cris's "Song of the Soul," with the whole audience linked arm in arm and singing and swaying together. As Marianne said, "The music fed the audience and the audience fed the music."

These concerts represented some of the best of who we were. Every aspect of the productions—sound, lights, staging, promotion—was skillfully handled by women. The performances were strong, the music soared, the lyrics portrayed women and women's lives in ways that were honest and touching, funny and inspirational. The local women's concert producers we worked with gave lobby space over to organizations representing and supporting the wide array of women's political activities. Together we created community.

On the other hand, the performers were all white and represented a particular kind of Women's Music—the kind we so did not want to be limited by. With very few exceptions, all the members of all the crews were white. Not surprisingly, most of the audience members were white. This was an issue that Olivia would address head-on fairly soon and with some success.

All of us who were involved in planning Women on Wheels wanted the process to reflect our feminist values as much as the product itself. We all assumed we shared the same values, and in the larger sense we probably did. But there were differences among us that led to some difficult and contentious meetings. For this tour our disagreements were primarily over the price of the concert tickets and whether any of the concerts would be designated "women-only."

We spent a lot of energy thinking/talking/writing/struggling about money. Most of us were pretty screwed up about money, and most of us didn't really know how to talk about it. Who could blame us? This was America, where the prevailing myth was that America was a classless society in which, with good character and a little effort, anyone could move up the ladder to more money and a better life. The only people who cared about "class" were communists or the British. Certainly not "normal" Americans. Here people got fired just for comparing their wages and salaries with coworkers. The message was clear—always best not to talk about money. For women—especially middle-class women—there was an additional obstacle. Taking care of the family finances was a man's job, and women were rarely encouraged or allowed to be in control of their own money. In fact, before 1974, a woman could only get a credit card in the name of her husband, and a woman without a husband usually had to bring a man with her to co-sign for the card.

There were so many strands of consciousness, or lack thereof, running through the movement. Many of the white, middle-class women who came from the Left felt shame about their class background and held in contempt the class values and aspirations they had been raised with. Calling someone or something "bourgeois" was almost as bad as calling them "male-identified." Many women romanticized working-class people and thought poverty was noble, and these folks were trying to move down the ladder rather than up. Most of the working-class women I knew were appalled by these attempts at downward mobility—there was nothing romantic for them about not having enough or not having access to the "right stuff." Some of the women with real wealth tried to hide it. They thought they would be drummed out of the movement if others found out. Some women actually got access to their fortunes and put money into various movement projects, but for the most part there was a lingering mistrust of them—they could always go back to their privileged way of life.

At Olivia we talked about money and class a lot. In an odd way, money was central to everything we did. We accepted it and refused to accept it, saw it as a tool to help us reach our goals and as the sword that hung over our heads. What else would you expect from revolutionaries trying to build a successful business—a business with a goal of overthrowing capitalism—in the middle of a system of advanced capitalism?

We wanted women, including ourselves, to be able to make a good living while making a better world. We struggled constantly with finding a balance between how high a value we placed on our work and how much money to charge for it because, although we didn't accept money as correct way to value anything, we had to buy groceries and pay rent and hire more women and produce more records, and all of these required cash. We tried to hold ourselves accountable to the women's community by regularly publishing our financial data, including album budgets. Jennifer and I wrote articles in the feminist press and did workshops all over the country on money. Sometimes we talked about feminist businesses in general, sometimes about the particulars of Olivia's finances and business principles; sometimes we got women talking about their attitudes about class and money. We wanted women to understand the deeper value of supporting women's businesses, and to stop expecting that Movement stuff would be free to Movement people. We also wanted to defend ourselves from charges of selling out because we were selling records and concerts for more than they cost.

So when the question of how much to charge for tickets to the Women on Wheels concerts came up, I was clear about what I thought was right—we should charge just enough to cover our expenses and pay the performers, producers, and crew a decent amount, and no more. Within those limitations, we should keep the ticket prices as low as we could. Holly and her rep were in agreement.

On the other side was Margie Adam. Margie wanted to charge more—basically as much as the market would bear, which was more than "just enough." Margie argued that to charge less was to devalue everyone's work. It was pretty unusual to be so bold in the pursuit of money in the Women's Movement. (Margie did not seem to have the shame or guilt that other women carried for having been born into privilege.)

We eventually compromised on a $4 ticket price, and, although we didn't acknowledge this at the time, I now think that we both had valid points. I wonder if our insistence on keeping prices down contributed to the undervaluing of women's work that was pretty rampant in the Women's Movement. Women would pay $25 (a high price) to see a conventional artist in concert but objected to paying $5 to see a Women's Music concert. Women expected to be ripped off by the mainstream but wouldn't tolerate it from their movement comrades, and for a lot of women it seemed that charging anything more than "just a little bit" constituted a rip-off.

In addition to the money issue, the Women on Wheels group struggled mightily over the "women-only" question, which was also playing out pretty much everywhere in all parts of the lesbian movement. Sometimes it seemed that there was a competition for "how separatist can you be?" But there was nothing game-like about how women dealt with the question; everyone was deadly serious and many felt that their lives really did depend on where other women stood on this issue. We had held this stance in The Furies. And we were not considered separatist enough by some because we still spoke to our fathers and brothers, our heterosexual mothers and sisters, and even had some contacts with the straight women's movement.

The distance between any of us and the people just to the left, or right, was infinitesimal compared to the distance between us and the patriarchs, or even the straight women's movement. But we focused an enormous amount of rage and fury at those closest to us. This horizontal hostility is not unusual among oppressed groups. For one thing, we have access to the people closest to us, and we don't have access to the ruling class or the politically powerful. For another, it is safer to go after people who cannot come after you with the power of the state behind them. Finally, I think that as each of us found our own voices and found our own groups, we developed and became fiercely attached to our own visions. We worked hard to develop our own politics out of this vision, and this set of politics—our analysis of how power worked, our goals and our values—became our "positions," and we defined ourselves by our positions. We were stuck in a binary world of right and wrong, female and male, lesbian and straight, feminist and male-identified, tough and soft.

We ignored or found a way to justify the contradictions within our politics. That Cris Williamson and Olivia Records stayed hooked up for so long is a perfect example. In the 1970s, Cris had not come out as a lesbian on stage, and her political statements focused on the health of the planet—which, at that time, we did not consider feminist or political. She preferred not to do women-only concerts, she would not meet with production collectives before and after her shows, and she didn't want to do workshops. Why could we tolerate this with Cris but not with others? In part, I think it was because we loved her music, she was willing to go with us as far as she could, and the whole idea of starting a record company was hers. And she wasn't taking "positions." For example, she wasn't refusing to come out because she was trying to reach a larger audience, as some artists claimed. She just didn't feel comfortable doing it, so even though we might talk about her internalized homophobia, she wasn't trying to advance a vision that was different from ours. We drove each other crazy, but we considered her *our* artist and she considered us *her* record company, and we were family.

In the larger movement, we didn't have the insight or the language to address our differences with understanding. We were not as interested in compromise as we were in winning, in being "right." And so these minor disagreements among people who basically agreed on almost everything became wedges that kept us at each other's throats and were part of the reason the movement eventually splintered.

This wasn't true for just Women on Wheels or Women's Music. There was a time in the mid '80s, after I had left Olivia, when feminist women were picketing one of the women's bookstores in the Bay Area; feminist women were organizing a boycott of one of the Women's Music festivals; and a lesbian who became a lawyer in order to defend lesbian mothers from losing their children in custody battles with ex-husbands instead found herself representing lesbians in contentious lawsuits against each other. And it was frequently the case that today's enemy was yesterday's friend and maybe even lover.

There were other dynamics at play as well. During the planning of Women on Wheels, there was often resistance to Marianne Schneller, who had come up with the idea for the tour and was the prime organizer. It was said that she had no real connection to Women's Music and was claiming a role that should have gone to someone else. (Who that someone else might have been was never articulated.) Unfortunately, this was a much-too-frequent dynamic among feminists: "I'm not doing whatever it is that you're doing, but it's going to give you some visibility/authority/power/exposure/love/acknowledgment that you shouldn't have because there's only so much to go around and if you get it I won't, so let me tear you down for daring to stand up, even though I'm not willing/capable to do what you're doing." Over and over again we saw women trashed by other women for trying to lead. In our righteous desire to be anti-authoritarian, we were too often viciously anti-leadership. Marianne was a soft-spoken woman with a vision, and she was willing to let herself be pushed into the background in order to get the shows on the road.

In the end, we made one of the Oakland concerts "especially for women"—a phrase I detested, but Margie and Boo would not accept "women only." Since we couldn't legally exclude men from the Oakland Auditorium, we went along. But I considered the "especially" phrase a liberal cop-out. Needless to say, there were women from one end of California to the other who were angry about something the tour did or didn't do. Petitions were circulated and demands were made to have women-only space, lower ticket prices, free tickets, and time on stage for various political groups to rally support for their causes, which we had decided against. Some women were furious that we had access to these big audiences and all we were doing was making music.

The arguing and fighting and bad feelings among the principals went on throughout the whole tour. People sitting in the audiences had no idea. The musicians and crew were professional, and everyone was able to put their feelings aside in order to do a great show.

The concerts got great reviews in the feminist press and even in some mainstream media. The tour gave a big boost to the careers of the four performers. Cris's *Changer* album had only been out a few months, and we were selling out of it at every concert. Meg's and Holly's albums did well, and Margie, who didn't have an album yet, let it be known that hers was on its way.

And then there were the personal dynamics. Meg was developing a friendship with Holly, and I was glad for that. Although she never said anything, I often wondered if Meg's involvement with me and with the Olivia collective stifled her in some way—had her focusing too much on politics and not enough on music—and I thought having another musician friend would be good for her. I had no reason to think it would be anything other than that.

13 HURTS LIKE THE DEVIL
Heartbreak

W HEN WOMEN ON WHEELS WAS over, Meg and I went to Laguna Beach for a three-day vacation, and when we came back we moved. The house next door to the original Olivia house had become vacant, and we grabbed it. We needed more space for ourselves and for the office. We were adding staff who would soon become collective members, and we were adding products that needed to be stored, with a bigger space for packing them up and shipping them out.

We decided that Meg and I would move into the new house. We would occupy two of the bedrooms and a little room off the kitchen. The front of the house, including a large living room, would become the new office. Meg and I slept on a heated waterbed that took days to warm up once it was filled, so, in the interim, we had set up camp on a very uncomfortable pull-out sofa in the little room.

On the first night in our new home, we were lying in our temporary bed just off the kitchen, watching *The Sound of Music* on TV. Though I had never seen the movie, I was bored. Meg was telling me something that Holly had told her. Lately, Meg was telling me a lot of things that Holly had told her.

I turned to her and asked half-jokingly, "Are you in love with Holly?" Silence.

Meg and me in front of the Olivia house in LA

She turned her face away from me and mumbled, "We've been sleeping together."

Did somebody just punch me in the stomach? Did my heart just become so heavy it fell out of my body? I wanted to throw up. I wanted to cry. I wanted to scream at Meg. I wanted to kill Julie Andrews. All I was able to do was turn off the TV.

I got out of bed and walked into the kitchen, where I kept my cigarettes and ashtray. Meg had asked me not to smoke in whatever room we were sleeping in, and up to now I had agreed. At this moment, however, I was not inclined to adhere to our agreements. I lit up and glowered at her. "When did this start?"

"A while ago. Just a few weeks. On the tour." She fanned the smoke away with her hand.

I scrunched up my face in disbelief. "You mean this was going on while we were on vacation together? Is that why you were always running off to take care of 'personal' business? Were you calling her?"

"Yes." I could barely hear her, but I could hear her.

"Did you sleep with her in our bed?"

She rolled her eyes. "No, of course not. I would never do that."
"Oh how very considerate of you." I blew more smoke in her direction. "Are you in love with her?"
"I don't know. I am very attracted to her. I don't know what else." She looked so pained, which just infuriated me. "You make me sick. Get out of this bed. I'm not sleeping with you. Go away. You're disgusting. You're a liar and a cheat and you make me sick. Get out of here."

Meg left the room. I had no idea where she slept that night, and I didn't care. I rolled a joint in the hopes that it would put me to sleep, which eventually it did.

When I woke up in the morning, I felt as though my whole world had collapsed. I just felt so heavy, so bereft, so deeply hurt. I tried to go about my day, being a person who never wanted to allow emotions to interfere with getting done whatever needed to be done, and that morning's task was going to the phone company office to order a new phone line for our house, another for the original house, and switching that number to the new Olivia office. I sat in the waiting area at the AT&T office feeling as miserable as I had ever felt in my life, and wondering if all the other people could see on my face what I was feeling. I wanted to start screaming, "My lover has just betrayed me! She is sleeping with another woman. A straight woman! How can you all just sit here as though nothing has happened?" Fortunately, I restrained myself. But when I finished with the phone company, I drove home and rounded up Judy and Jennifer. Kate was out.

I asked them to join me at our eating table in the first Olivia house. I reached into a cabinet and pulled out a bottle of Scotch. It was a fifth of J&B with the distinctive red and yellow label. I opened the bottle and took a slug. I hardly ever drank alcohol. They stared at me. "Meg is sleeping with Holly." I passed the bottle to Jennifer, who took a drink and passed it to Judy. For the next hour or so, we sat at the table and proceeded to drink from the bottle until it was empty. I ranted. They were indignant on my behalf, and their own. Jennifer later told me that she thought it was "a family tragedy and more than we could handle. It was so hard because we lived and worked together and were so dependent on each other." We got louder and more rowdy, and then we alternately threw up and passed out. I have never been so drunk in my life. There is nothing about the experience that I ever want to repeat.

Over the next three months, I tried to make peace with Meg. I even tried to be friends with Holly, but we were both much too wary and nervous about being in each other's presence. I didn't understand what she was thinking when she began the sexual relationship with Meg. Was she thinking? Did she think this is what lesbians do? I didn't want to fight with her, so I never asked her. I wasn't as angry with her as I was with Meg because Holly had made no commitments to me; she was not crafting a life with me, but Meg was. I wasn't angry with Holly. Just disgusted.

I was determined that this was not going to interfere with the functioning of Olivia or with my ability to continue booking and traveling with Meg. I was unaware of how this was affecting the rest of the Olives, but Jennifer later told me that Meg's relationship with Holly was very threatening. "It threatened our trust, our tight bond, our ability to count on one another—and most of all, it threatened you and what you were trying to do. Your leadership was so critical to the whole enterprise. If you went down, it could all go down."

When we first got together, Meg and I had agreed that we would be monogamous, but even though she had broken her promise to me, I believed that, as a feminist, I should be able to abide this new arrangement. I was appalled and ashamed that I felt jealous, that I wished Holly ill, that I was so angry at Meg. I found it unacceptable that my emotions had such a hold on me—especially these emotions that seemed to belong to patriarchal ideas of ownership and sexual propriety. The women of Olivia had a materialistic view of the world. We believed that the "negative" emotions—with the exception of anger—belonged to the territory that women were supposed to inhabit, and we wanted none of it. When we were frightened or sad, our attitude was "just deal with it." We considered ourselves revolutionaries trying to live out our values and our vision of a just society. In the process of inventing the new world, we rejected everything that smacked of the "traditional" and especially, what Jennifer called the "unbrave." We truly believed that we would overthrow the patriarchy and capitalism, that we would avoid or destroy all obstacles, that the clarity and purity of our vision would enable us to do whatever needed to be done. We had started a record company without knowing the first thing about how to do that, hadn't we?

So I tried mightily to act as if everything was just fine. But everything was not fine. Try as I might, this stoical face I showed the world was just a façade and did nothing to soothe my broken heart. In addition, the betrayal I felt went deeper than my lover sleeping with another woman. There was a fundamental breach of what I considered a primary value of feminism—that we would be honest with each other.

After three months, I realized I couldn't go on "sharing" Meg, and I told her I wanted to end our relationship. She didn't argue. There was a small apartment building across the street from our houses, and I moved in. We tried to be civil to each other. We wanted to continue working together. I had no intention of leaving Olivia—my political work was always top of my priorities, more important than relationships or feelings or health.

The reaction of the lesbian community was just more salt in the wound. Once Meg and I were officially Not Together, word got out. Women were ecstatic—Holly Near had come out! Meg and Holly were a couple! They began to sit in on each other's gigs in LA and whenever they happened to be performing in the same town. Audiences greeted them rapturously, as though they had just overthrown the patriarchy. There were expectations that Holly would start writing songs and speaking directly to her mainly Lefty audience about lesbianism, and she did. A lot of folks in that audience were not so thrilled initially, afraid that she would desert the causes of peace and social justice in favor of lesbian feminism, as though they were not part of the same whole. But Holly never backed off. She even wrote a song called "You Bet" which defended the singing of love songs to women as a political act. They started writing songs together, and decided they wanted to tour together.

There was no way I was going to take that on, so Jennifer worked with Holly's manager/booking agent and put together their tour.

I struggled constantly with my feelings. I would sit in collective meetings and glare at Meg or criticize her for something she said that I could call racist or classist or insufficiently feminist. It would never be "personal." In the office, I would try to ignore her, and if I couldn't do that, I would try to speak to her in a neutral tone, which just sounded like English was my, or her, second language. We no longer spoke to each other in the language we had invented for ourselves.

Another problem was that Meg was an active alcoholic and I was deeply codependent. It was so hard for us to break out of our patterns of relating to each other while we continued to see each other almost every day and work together on what was essentially our baby. We kept trying to be friends, and we kept hurting each other. We had no models to look to. We saw lesbian couples breaking up and not speaking to each other, sometimes dividing the community into sides. It didn't help at all that Meg drowned her feelings in bottles of wine, and I did everything I could to not feel mine.

The great irony is that I understood completely the power of emotion. Our decision to use music as the means to promulgate our message—instead of publishing political theory and lesbian feminist thought as we had in *The Furies*—resulted from our belief that the heart has its own intelligence. I just wouldn't acknowledge that in myself.

I finally broke down and went to two sessions with a feminist therapist—something I thought was only for weak women who couldn't reason their way out of their troubles. My therapist taught me how to say "no" to Meg, and this was a big step for me. I had to learn how to stop taking care of her because now when I did, I just ended up resenting her more. I began to be able to put some distance between us, and I began dating other women, and I liked many of them—and am still friends with some—but I was pretty lonely. I also smoked a lot of dope.

I continued with Olivia for another four years, but something fundamental changed for me. I held on to the vision and I was passionate about the work, but now I walked through my days with a broken heart.

I don't know if it is still the case today, but in the '70s and '80s there were many women's and lesbian enterprises/businesses/projects that were created by women who were lovers and partners. Diana Press, the Oakland Women's Press Collective, the Women's Philharmonic, A Woman's Place Bookstore, to name just a few. What was it about our relationships that unleashed so much creative energy? I didn't see this happening among heterosexual couples or gay men, so what was it? And what happened to it? Did all that energy dissipate when lesbians started having babies?

Meg and I were together for four years and it took me four years to get over her, but I did, and she did, and today, although we have followed very different paths, we are great friends, once again speaking our private language, still calling each other B's, the shortened version of BC's.

14 Hoodoo'd

But We Go On and Make *BeBe K'Roche*

I N THE 1970s IN THE Bay Area, and, really, all up and down the West Coast, women's bands flourished. Like lesbian couples, the bands formed and unformed. Lovers would organize a band, play together for some months or even years, and when the original couple broke up, the band might split up and die or reconstitute itself with a new player. The woman you saw playing bass with one band last week might be the guitarist in another this week. There were lesbian bars and women's coffee houses, and even some daring male-owned clubs, that booked the bands for a percentage of the door, or a $20 guarantee, plus whatever the band could collect in tips. In this way, musicians could scratch out a bare living. Among them were High Risk in Los Angeles, the Clinch Mountain Backsteppers in Portland, and, in the Bay Area, Sweet Chariot, Lizzy Tisch, Alive!, the Berkeley Women's Music Collective, and a rock band called BeBe K'Roche.

The Olivia collective was ensconced in LA considering our next move. The Women on Wheels tour had been a huge success, playing to more than ten thousand people—mostly women—in a two-week period. The albums of Cris and Meg were selling beyond our expectations. After almost every concert, I had to drive back to Los Angeles and load up the car with more boxes of *Changer* and *I Know You Know* to deliver to the local distributor.

We didn't know what we wanted to do next but we knew we didn't want to do what we had already done. If we meant what we said about Women's Music being everything that women were, we needed to start representing that. And then we received a tape and letter in the mail from Subie Baker, our Bay Area distributor. "Check out this band," the letter said. "They are tight and good and lesbians and very popular up here." This was BeBe K'Roche.

Peggy Mitchell (bass) and Tiik Pollet (guitar) were lovers when they started the band. Tiik explains on her website where the name came from:

> I made up the name BeBe K'Roche one day when Peggy and I were at home relaxing with some herbal tea and found a baby cockroach in the bottom of Peggy's cup. In a mock French accent and attempt to lessen the gross shock value I quipped, 'Ah!!! Look at ze bebe cock roche.' A sense of humor and a passion for numerology turned this into the band name, BeBe K'Roche, which equals the number eleven. Voila! A band was born.

Peggy and Tiik convinced Virginia Rubino (lead vocals and keyboards) to move up from LA, where she had been part of High Risk. Jake Lampert came on as the drummer while also playing with the Berkeley Women's Music Collective. For a while, Peggy and Virginia and some other women lived together in a house in Berkeley with a sign above the entrance that said "No Men, No Meat, No Monogamy." But then Peggy fell in love with Kim Johnson, and Tiik left the band. Jerene Jackson replaced her on guitar. The band needed a manager, and so in the spirit of the time, Kim, who had absolutely no experience in this arena, took on the job. She got them a fairly steady gig at the White Horse, a lesbian and gay bar in Oakland, and at other clubs and bars within a few hours' drive of the Bay Area, from Cotati to Santa Cruz. Nobody was getting rich, but everybody was paying the rent and making music.

We loved the music on the tape that Subie sent. We thought that this could be the breakaway sound we were looking for, and it wasn't just their music that broke the mold of established Women's Music. They were edgy and flamboyant on stage and even in person. Virginia in particular had a style that in earlier days might have been called "bohemian" but now just seemed wild. She was short and skinny and pugnacious and had a huge amount of energy. She had the powerful voice of a soul or blues singer, and she wrote most of the band's songs. Virginia was the center of the band. She never went anywhere without her equally skinny dog, Arrow. They were white and all of them had grown up in varying degrees of poverty. Their circle of friends and support was racially mixed, and they were comfortable with women of color in ways that we were not.

We didn't know it right away, but several band members were already using heavy drugs. Even if we had known I doubt that would have bothered us. We saw them as a very good band that would help us move Olivia and Women's Music and the Women's Movement in a new, more inclusive direction. They saw us as a bunch of middle-class women with a lot of power who could get them national prominence, lots of well-paying tours, and an easier way to live as musicians. Unfortunately, it didn't work out for them or for us.

Still, they were thrilled when we asked them to make a record. In one of our first meetings, they said they wanted Linda Tillery to produce their album. Judy and I looked at each other uneasily. "Who is Linda Tillery?" I asked. Now *they* looked uneasily at each other.

Kim, trying hard to be a "manager," did most of the talking at this point. "Very well-known and beloved Bay Area musician. She fronts a group called The Loading Zone. Incredible voice."

"She's a friend and we think she understands our music," Virginia chimed in.

"She'll make us better," Peggy added. "We know she will."

Judy asked, "She does rock?"

"Noooo," Kim stretched out the word so it took a good five seconds to say. "R&B, funk, soul."

"Has she ever produced a record before?"

"Listen," Virginia was getting agitated, "that doesn't matter. She has great chops. She's a real musician. She's spent plenty of time in the studio. And we trust her."

Judy and I were not as resistant as we might have seemed—just cautious, and a little nervous. Like the BeBes, we were entering new territory. We wanted to do right by them, but we also wanted to do right by ourselves. The fact that Linda had never produced an album was hardly a deal-breaker for us. It actually made her a little more attractive; here we had an opening to put one of our principles into action—giving women opportunities to create and learn and grow and discover their strengths and abilities. We asked Kim to set up a meeting for us. She did, and we couldn't have been happier with the result.

Linda is a big woman, standing around 5' 10", with dark brown skin and, at that time, a full Afro. She displayed a sharp intelligence about the music business that we lacked. Linda had heard BeBe K'Roche play around town and thought they had a good sound and played well together. She thought producing their album would be a good stretch and an important step for her. The band had already worked out the songs they wanted on the album, so Linda didn't have to choose the material or figure out their parts or hire many backup players. Instead, she thought she would really get to use her ears to help them get the best sound they could on every note, in every song. We talked about budgets, studios, engineers. More than getting along, we really liked each other. We wrote up contracts and made arrangements.

We were still living in LA, but the band would record in San Francisco. We had recently been introduced to a very experienced engineer who knew her way around bands and complex recordings. Her name was Sandy Stone, and she was as anxious to work with us as we were with her. This made the band very happy. They had had too many performances in which the sound person didn't know how to mic or mix a band. Knowing they had a crackerjack engineer and their first choice as producer was gold. They recorded in May of 1976.

I didn't get to many of the recording sessions, but I got to enough to get a whiff of what was going on. The control room smelled like an Italian deli. Someone had decided—I think it was Virginia—that everyone would stay healthy if they ate a clove of garlic with their lunchtime sandwich every day. Pretty soon they had dumped the sandwiches, and everyone just nibbled on raw garlic during the sessions. It was a test put to each of the Olives when we dropped into a recording session. I loved garlic, so no problem, although after a few days of this I started having digestive issues. Luckily, it was almost time for me to go back to LA. But I did get to have one of those moments that let me know we were doing the right thing.

The band was recording "Kahlua Mama," the song that Linda and everyone thought would be the hit. In the middle of a take, Linda asked Sandy to stop recording, to turn off the mics and to turn off the lights in the studio. She walked out of the control room, into the studio, and whispered something in Virginia's ear. They walked behind a six-foot-high baffle that was pushed off to one side. After about five minutes, they emerged. Linda came back into the control room and signaled

Sandy that she could start. The band resumed and they laid down a great version. I asked Linda what she was doing with Virginia behind the baffle. "I wanted to teach her a vocal lick that I thought would be perfect in the song."

Just that. I was so happy. Here was this little microcosm of women getting to do things they had never done before and helping each other and teaching each other and being kind to each other. Linda told me that Sandy had been like that with her. Sandy was eager to be helpful and really taught her a lot. She answered her questions and volunteered useful information about mics and sound placement and other technical aspects of recording that made Linda a better producer and a better studio musician herself.

I had other moments with the band that were not quite so full of grace and displayed the limitations of my white, middle-class background. They were using all kinds of African and Latin percussion instruments that I had never heard of, like a virbraslap, güiro, kalimba and agogô. One afternoon, when we were discussing the album jacket and what kind of photos they wanted on the back cover, I suggested it would be great to have a photo of all the percussion because I saw this as a good way to teach women about these instruments. Peggy gave me a look that made me feel like I was the least cool person in the universe. They wanted to make a record album, not an educational experience.

At another point, I asked Virginia the meaning of the opening line of "Kahlua Mama."

> Wing top memory
> It's for you the love pours forth
> And heats my body, and heats my body
> Oh such inspiration
> I'm a lonely woman without you

I'd like to lie with you forever
On some dark-like crown of mountain
Oh woman, oh woman
Oh Kahlua Mama, oh Kahlua Mama

I loved the image of "wing top memory" but I had never done well with metaphors.

Squinting her eyes to make sure the question had come from an actual human being, Virginia said she didn't know and it didn't matter. I felt again that I had wandered into a foreign land where I didn't understand the language or the customs. That didn't stop me from learning how to make Kahlua from scratch and having it be my beverage of choice for a while.

I loved the record. I didn't just love that it represented such a significant departure from our previous records. I really loved the music. While we waited for test pressings and actual physical albums, I carried a cassette with me and listened to it constantly. We released the album in October with an eye on Christmas sales. Almost none of our distributors had heard the band and asked me for help in estimating their initial orders. I figured out how many copies of *Changer* they had sold in the first two months of its release, and suggested that be their first order for *BeBe*. Women had been asking us for music they could dance to, and I was confident that this record would begin to satisfy that longing. We hoped and believed that the Olivia brand (although we never would have used that term, and I can hardly even write it now) would be enough to get women to the dances and concerts and into the record stores. We thought the music and the musicians didn't matter as much as the community, the politics, the vision.

Lisa Vogel, who was in the throes of planning the second year of the Michigan Womyn's Music Festival, booked a spring tour for the band. Kim would road-manage. Jerene had decided she didn't want to go on the road. The band needed a guitarist, and Robin Flower, who was playing with Clinch Mountain Backsteppers, auditioned and got the job. We had budgeted a whopping $1,000 for promotion—far more than we had allocated for either of the previous albums, but Meg and Cris were known, and, outside of the Bay Area, BeBe K'Roche was not. The band decided to use the money to buy a van. The one they had been using was not big enough to carry the four musicians (Virginia, Jake, Peggy, and Robin), Kim the manager, Karen their sound woman, all their equipment, and Arrow. This was not what we had in mind for promotion—we were thinking long-distance phone calls (which were expensive then), concert posters, ads in the feminist press, maybe even some radio ads. One of our core principles was that musicians should control every aspect of their records. We didn't agree with their decision, but it was theirs to make.

The tour was successful in some ways, disappointing in others—in turn demanding, crazy, revealing, and scary. These city girls found themselves in towns in the middle of the country that were not like the Bay Area. If there were identifiable (to other lesbians) lesbian bars, they were well hidden and called "members only," and women did not dare congregate in their parking lots. They almost had to sneak into their own clubs. The band members were used to being out and raucous and stoned. They dressed like dykes or hippies or both. After one late-night gig in Oklahoma, Kim, who was from the Midwest and had a better sense of the vibe, decided they should get out of town in a hurry.

The band played in straight clubs and in concerts/dances produced by the Women's Music circuit. They drew some good crowds of mostly younger women. Women danced and seemed to have a good time, but the band encountered some resistance. Robin Flower said, "We played loud, and a lot of women didn't like loud." They also played sexy. When they were on stage they played with a lawless, almost punk, attitude, but they were serious musicians, and they mostly liked playing with each other. But unlike the concerts of the soloists, at the end of the show people didn't flock to the lobby to buy records.

The last stop on their tour was the 4th National Women's Music Festival in Champaign–Urbana, Illinois, a three- or four-day festival held at the University of Illinois. Playing at the NWMF was a great opportunity for an unknown band to introduce themselves to women from all over the country. For BeBe K'Roche, it was a disaster. The six women (and Arrow) had essentially been living together in very close quarters for months; some of them were shooting up regularly; tensions were inevitable. Virginia and Jake spent a good part of their concert sniping at each other off mic. This would be their last performance.

By the end of 1977, 14 months after its release, *BeBe K'Roche* had sold fewer than 9,500 records. Perhaps this band was just not hitting the right chords with the women's communities, and another band would do better. But I worried that there was something else afoot. So many women had told us how the music of Meg and Cris spoke to them. What was it about BeBe that didn't? Their songs were woman-centered, they spoke about love between women, about change, about challenges that women face. Was it the music, then? The appearance and presentation of the musicians? Were we only going to be successful with charismatic folk musicians? Could our predominantly white, middle-class audience only relate to women who looked like them? Could they not connect with the African and African American-rooted sound?

I understand that everyone has her own musical taste, her own likes and dislikes. But I thought—hoped, really—that because it was an *Olivia* record, women would buy it to support

Olivia. We saw Olivia as building and serving our community, but it seemed that much of the community was not as interested in building community as they were in satisfying their own musical hunger. Women loved the *idea* of this national women's record company, this burgeoning world of Women's Music, but not enough to lay out a few dollars for an album that didn't move them. We would later hear from women that rock music—indeed, anything that wasn't folk music—was "male." I found this deeply dispiriting and a great disappointment.

One of the lessons we drew from this experience was that, if we were going to record unknown artists, we needed to do a much better job of marketing them. Olivia-love would not be enough to motivate women to buy records.

Another lesson was that gifts don't always come in the expected package. Meeting and working with Linda Tillery was the unexpected blessing of the whole experience. This would be the beginning of a very important relationship for me and for Linda and for Olivia.

15 DON'T SAY SISTER (UNTIL YOU MEAN IT)

Who Is the Enemy? Who Is the Sister?

L ATE FEBRUARY 1976. MEG AND HOLLY were continuing their "affair" or "relationship" or whatever they were calling it. I was calling it heart-breakingly, gut-wrenchingly horrible. But never one to let my emotions interfere with my work, I booked a tour for Meg for the Northwest for March and April. Largely because of the Women on Wheels Tour, Olivia was starting to get noticed in the mainstream music press, with articles in *Rolling Stone*, *Crawdaddy*, and a cover piece in *Billboard* with the headline "Fems Only at Olivia Label." We thought this was pretty funny—*Billboard* calling us "fems" because we were women, whereas at least some of us were proudly butch. We enjoyed putting on some fake-righteous indignation over this one. We hoped the excitement generated by Women on Wheels and all the feminist- and mainstream-media coverage would carry over and bring larger audiences to Meg's concerts. We had no idea there would be backlash as well.

Meg and I drove up the coast and on into Canada, doing concerts in Portland, Vancouver, and other cities. One of the last shows was to be at the Seattle Women's Coffee Coven. We were not looking forward to it. One day, while we were on the road, Jennifer had answered the phone at the Olivia office and found herself being blasted by a group calling themselves the Seattle Separatists. They were furious at Olivia, furious at Meg, and generally furious.

They told Jennifer that Olivia was selling out lesbians, that the music we were producing, both on records and in concert, was not challenging male supremacy in any way, but was just carving out a slightly bigger closet for lesbians to live in. In a most strident tone, they started reading from an article called "Lesbians in Revolt" that said, in part:

> Being a Lesbian is part of challenging male supremacy but not the end …. As the question of homosexuality has become public, reformists define it as a private question of who you sleep with in order to sidetrack our understanding of the politics of sex. For the Lesbian feminist it is not private; it is a political matter of oppression, domination and power.

Jennifer interrupted. "Wait a minute," she had to shout over them to be heard. "You're reading from *The Furies*. Are you aware that many of us in the Olivia collective were part of The Furies collective? That we wrote that stuff?"

There was some mumbling in the background, and then, "Well, you all have drifted far away from it. You all should go back and re-read what you wrote." And then they let her know that they wanted to meet with Meg and me when we got to Seattle. Jennifer conveyed the message to us with a warning that these women seemed dangerous to her, that their level of anger seemed way out of proportion to whatever—crime?—we might have committed. We could only speculate on what the danger might be: Would they block women from getting in the door? Heckle Meg from the audience? Storm the stage and try to shut the concert down? My anxiety grew.

On the night of Meg's Seattle concert, they stood in front of the Coffee Coven and passed out leaflets, headlined "Politics or Mush":

> Olivia Records (the company Meg Christian records with) has appeared to be dealing with politics in an unconscious way but has in fact made a deliberate choice. They have decided not to further lesbian political development but to sell the largest number of records to the largest number of women possible. In order to do this they have had to pervert lesbian culture into the heterosexual mode of romantic mush.
>
> Meg Christian sings mush. Mush is roMANce, idealization, the search for true love, for 'her,' and the pain of losing that search.
>
> Mush is often mistaken or substituted for love or other emotions. Instead of feeling what we're feeling about each other we fit it into Romeo and Juliet. All love and relationships are measured up to storybook ideals. And no one can, or should meet them....
>
> We want culture that reflects and affirms our politics as lesbian separatists. Culture that reflects and affirms the politics of the straight women's movement or a vaguely-defined 'lesbian-feminist' movement is not clearly anti-patriarchal or pro-lesbian, and is alienating to us.

The fact that Meg's Seattle concert was designated women-only was not enough. Allowing our artists to be interviewed by and our albums reviewed in "male media such as *The Rolling Stone* [*sic*] is participating in, rather than fighting, the patriarchal system."

It felt awful to be seen like this by separatists. Most of the time it was the non-separatists who were on our case—women who wanted to know why we wouldn't work closely with straight women or let men into our concerts. Here, again, was this problem that seemed endemic to the Women's Movement. We took on those closest to us, separating ourselves into smaller and smaller factions each more "radical" than the next, each more "correct." I had been a prime example of this myself as part of The Furies collective. Even now, although Olivia had moved away from the stances advocated by the Seattle Separatists, we drew our own lines. We were dismissive of women who made music with men or used male distributors. We were all so attached to what our positions said about us. And now I wonder, what *did* they say about us?

Meg and I agreed to meet with the Seattle Separatists and talk things over. We placed value on accessibility and account-ability, and we often sat with our concert producers—usually a feminist collective—after Meg's concerts and listened to their feedback. So, in spite of my anger at not being seen as a revo-lutionary fighter and my belief that the Seps were *not* tearing down the patriarchy by tearing down Olivia, I was willing to sit with them. We had several hours to kill before our meeting, and we went to a coffee shop and amused ourselves with a new electronic game we had never seen before, called Pong. Batting the digital icon back and forth and pretending it was somebody's head helped relieve some of the tension we felt.

There were eight of them and the two of us, all sitting on the floor in a circle in somebody's living room. They all wore a variation on the theme of overalls and flannel shirts. Meg was wearing light blue drawstring pants and a long-sleeve navy T-shirt. I was moderately dressed up, wearing khaki cords and a black sweatshirt.

They began with an apology. There had been a scuffle in front of the Coffee Coven between some women who were not part of their group but were supporters and women who wanted to enter the coffee house. The concert-goers had felt harassed and violated. Some women had turned around and gone home.

"These women were not Seattle Separatists, but I know that our leafleting your concert let them think that driving women away was what we wanted. It wasn't. We're sorry."

This was so not what we expected that we were disarmed and relaxed a little.

The Sep went on. "We appreciate that you're willing to meet with us. A lot of other musicians who have come through Seattle haven't been."

Meg, who rarely spoke in these encounters, said, "Well, I can understand why. You don't know what it takes to do a concert, how much of myself I put out there, and you all seem so hostile. It's scary."

I lit up a cigarette and added, "You do seem to have missed the point of what we're doing, what we're trying to do. I mean, really, if you think that we are supporting patriarchy and not supporting lesbians, I think we're not living in the same world."

A Sep named Susan spoke up. "'Valentine Song' is a good example, or, really, a bad example. Valentine's Day is just a Hallmark Holiday designed to get people to spend money on cards and candy and to make women who don't have a 'valentine' feel shitty about themselves. And your song supports that."

Meg rolled her eyes. "Are you against love? The song is about love, not about buying cards."

Susan started jabbing her finger at Meg. "Oh, come on. 'Dining and dancing?' That's not what dykes do. Dykes don't 'dine.' Sure, you have women loving each other, but so what? You're just perpetuating the same lies about romantic love."

I could hardly stay sitting down. "Wait a minute. Haven't you ever been in love? What have you got against romance? I love being in love. What's wrong with celebrating that?"

The Sep named Elaine started yelling. "It's not political! It's just a fairy tale."

I yelled back. "But it's how we feel! It's how Meg felt when she wrote the song."

"Because you are buying into the patriarchal bullshit. And calling it 'dining' is a dead giveaway. It's classist. Working class women *eat*."

Meg was beside herself. "Art!" she shouted. It sounds better to say 'dining and dancing'! Alliteration! It's a song! It's not a manifesto!"

And that, of course, was the problem.

We spent the next two hours going back and forth, dissecting the lyrics to Meg's songs, the raps she did before her songs, my Olivia rap, their leaflet and other statements they had made about Olivia. At one point, they accused us of pandering to heterosexuals and warned us that those women would never be our allies. Referring to the Women on Wheels tour, and not knowing that Meg had brought Holly out, they said, "Do you really think that if Holly Near understood Lesbian separatism she would have anything to do with you?" Ha. But in the end, we actually had some movement. I'm not sure how it happened. Maybe we wore each other out. Whatever it was, there was a moment when we started to hear each other a little better.

Meg agreed to be more explicit on stage about the political nature of coming out. I agreed to talk more about male privilege in my Olivia rap. They agreed to stop slamming Olivia in the lesbian press. There were hugs all around and we left for our next concert in Portland. But we both felt sick to our stomachs. There was just something nauseating about the whole process. And it would be repeated in other forms, around other issues, throughout my years with Olivia.

We did not understand or value the concept of calling people in—seeing them as potential comrades and allies who could be brought inside the circle with kindness—instead of always calling them out—using harsh language to point out their mistakes and the flaws in their positions. Too often we felt that in order to do our work, it was necessary to draw lines and create distance between ourselves and others. This was true of the entire progressive movement—from the Black Panther Party and SDS to the National Organization for Women. We were each pursuing our own dream and believed that anyone who was not pursuing our dream with our values—while they might not be an enemy, they surely were not an ally. We expended huge amounts of energy criticizing and often vilifying each other. Victories come more easily when you're fighting someone your own size. We thought our encounter with the Seattle Separatists was a big deal, but it was really nothing more than a kerfuffle compared to what came after.

I don't know exactly when it happened, but a few months later, in a letter to a friend, I wrote:

> We are no longer calling ourselves separatists partly because the word separatism means so many different things to everybody, partly because it is seeming more and more obvious to us that the separatist movement is a white middle class movement. Its inability to develop a strategy that includes Third World and working class women; its demands that all women work with women only and those who don't are the enemy; its refusal to deal constructively with any alternatives that deal with economics or the daily lives of most women, make us feel like we can't support that position any more, even if we mean something different by the word. We are starting the process of including Third World women in our collective—women who are dykes, feminists, political, and who cannot consider separatism because

they cannot trust the women's movement to deal with racism. And that makes absolute sense to me.

I had to let go of calling myself, seeing myself, as a separatist, and it wasn't easy. There was a glamour to being thought of as part of the radical fringe and I liked it. But there were other parts of my dream that were stronger now, and that's where I wanted to go.

16 WHEN ANGER TAKES THE WHEEL

Hiring Sandy Stone

I N THE MIDDLE OF RECORDING BeBe K'Roche, we learned we
had another problem that would *not* be resolved with hugs
all around, and that would put us in the center of a storm
that is still ravaging the women's community. When we started
working with Sandy Stone, we thought we were incredibly lucky
to have found a woman engineer with her huge amount and
variety of recording experience, someone who wasn't attached
to a particular studio and could come and go as she wanted.
And what she wanted was to work with Olivia when we had
records to make, and to help us build our own studio when we
weren't cutting a record. What could be better?

Forty years later, the repercussions of our decision to hire
Sandy still reverberate among feminists and lesbians.

In 1976, the term "trans woman" didn't exist, but that's what
she was. The term then was "male-to-female transsexual," what
today, with more understanding, is called AMAB—assigned
male at birth. Sandy was a recording engineer with exceptional
credentials and experience, having worked with Jimi Hendrix,
Velvet Underground, the Grateful Dead, Jefferson Airplane,
and dozens of others in rock royalty. She gave up that scene in
part because she was sick of the drug craziness that was domi-
nating recording sessions, and also because she was beginning

her transition from male to female and didn't think her rock buddies would be supportive. She lived in Santa Cruz and was part of a collective of women called TranSisters that sold and repaired audio gear. She did occasional recording sessions when the music moved her and the people involved seemed mellow.

By the end of 1975, when we knew that *BeBe K'Roche* would be our next album, we knew we would need to find a new engineer. As much as we loved Joan Lowe, we had come to understand she didn't have the chops for this project. And, as it turned out, she knew it too. After *Changer* was finished, Judy met with her and explained that we needed an engineer with experience in multi-track recording and working with bands. Joan neither argued nor questioned Judy, just nodded her head in understanding. But still...a sad parting.

So we started to ask around for other women engineers, and Patrick Gleeson, the owner of Different Fur, a San Francisco recording studio, suggested Sandy Stone. Judy drove up to Santa Cruz with a couple of members of BeBe K'Roche to talk to her and make sure her style would be compatible with the band's and Olivia's. Sandy didn't reveal that she was transgender and neither Judy nor the BeBes had any idea. They came back convinced we had found a new engineer to work with.

However, before we started working together, we learned from Boo Price that Sandy was transgender. Boo was currently producing Margie's first album, and they were recording it at Different Fur. Patrick must have told Boo that Sandy was transgender, and Boo called and told me.

Many hours were spent in collective meetings deciding what to do. On the one hand, Sandy was not "really" a woman in the sense we'd been defining the word. On the other, she was no longer "really" a man. We were dismissive of men who called themselves feminist and wanted to be part of the Women's Movement. "Give up your privilege," we would say to them, "and then we'll talk about whether you are feminists." Sandy had clearly given up whatever male privilege she had. A heterosexual, white, male, well-paid studio engineer who had hobnobbed with the rock music elite, she had given it all up in order to transition. And now, she was willing to throw in with us: to earn the pittance that we paid, to work with musicians with little or no studio experience, to be accountable to a collective of radical lesbian feminists. And she stayed in relationship with her woman lover.

Did that make her a lesbian? A feminist? A woman?

We didn't know how to answer those questions. There was no transgender movement in 1976, no literature on trans people that we were aware of, no "queer theory" or "gender studies" departments. Indeed, women's studies was just getting its foot in the door of academia. There were no discussions about transgender people in the feminist press. And, given the controversy stirred up by something as innocent as Meg's love songs from the likes of the Seattle Separatists, we didn't have confidence that we could have a constructive dialogue about these questions in the lesbian community. I'm not even sure that we knew what a reasonable conversation about big political differences would look or sound like.

In the meantime, we had a band that was ready to record and an engineer who was willing and able to do it and who we felt confident would deliver the quality we were committed to. We decided we would work with Sandy on this album and see if we were a good fit.

Although we didn't hide the fact that we were working with a trans woman engineer, we didn't broadcast it either. But soon the news was all over the lesbian and feminist communities. Many lesbians were furious and disgusted. They wouldn't speak to Sandy, but they let Olivia know exactly how they felt. They sent back Olivia records they had purchased, sometimes smashed into pieces. They wrote hate-filled letters accusing us of being in cahoots with the patriarchy; they said we had seduced them with our righteous words and music only to show our true colors once we had hooked them; they said we were worse than men because at least men were honest about their contempt for women. They sent statements of outrage signed by dozens of women to the feminist press. Musicians denounced us from the stage, claiming we should drop the "women's" from "national women's record company."

This was painful for us, and I can only imagine how painful it was for Sandy. She didn't speak much about how she was feeling—she seemed to be of the stiff-upper-lip school, but she did get a little more quiet around us. The rest of us reacted defensively. Their rage and disdain and our defensiveness left no room for discussion. But when a group of lesbians from the San Francisco Bay Area asked to meet with us to discuss their concerns, we agreed, hoping that we would be able to reason together, believing that our integrity as feminists could not be questioned, that the work we had done, the community we were helping to build and the movement we were helping to inspire clearly put us on the same side. The meeting would take place the day after a concert we were producing at the Oakland Auditorium on a Saturday night in December of 1976. We thought the discussion would focus on Sandy. We didn't know that it would be that and more. Much, much more.

The headliner at the concert was Teresa Trull, whose album we would release in a few months. Teresa was performing with a band including Jerene Jackson on electric guitar, Diane Lindsay on electric bass, and Linda Tillery on drums. We had recently decided that we were going to move to Oakland later the following year, and we were offering this concert as a gift to our prospective community. On stage, Teresa was bouncing around, thoroughly enjoying playing with the band. On the few numbers where she just accompanied herself on acoustic guitar, she seemed shy and slightly frightened by all the attention. But the audience of close to fifteen hundred seemed enchanted with her no matter what she did.

Who were not enchanted were the women we met with the next day. The meeting was on the second floor of Old Wives' Tales, the feminist bookstore in San Francisco. There must have been fifty women, arrayed in a circle—a lot of women we didn't know, many we did, some of whom we had had nothing but positive relationships with. We had asked a few friends and allies to come, women we knew were supportive of our working with Sandy. The Olives in attendance were Judy, Kate, Jennifer, Sandy Stone, Teresa, Sandy Ramsey, and me. (Meg was on the road.) We walked into a room so thick with hostility that it was smothering. But we were brave, and we walked in smiling and greeting everyone.

The meeting began with the reading of a prepared statement by one of the women who had called the meeting. The essence of the statement was that it was common knowledge that the very act of becoming transgender was destructive and that trans women were really men and very male and would destroy the Women's Movement. She asked if we had a response. Her voice shaking, Sandy just said, "Bullshit." At this point, Sandy was asked to leave the room. Several of us started to object, but Sandy was glad to go. "I would rather eat glass than spend another minute with these people," she said as she gathered her belongings and stormed out. The rest of us then decided that we would each take a turn sitting outside the room with Sandy. It would have been smarter if we had all left at that point. Instead, for the next several hours, we listened to women who considered themselves lesbian feminists rip into us. Sandy Stone was the excuse, but the list of grievances was much longer.

Several women went off on the music at the Teresa Trull concert the night before, calling it "cock rock." They said that playing music with electric guitars and drums made us no different than the Rolling Stones.

Others accused us of abandoning the feminist bookstores and coffeehouses, which could typically hold forty to one hundred people, and supporting the patriarchy by having the concert at the two-thousand-seat Oakland Auditorium.

One woman was furious about our failure to have recorded any music from Central European Jews and saw this as a sign of gross anti-Semitism.

That was followed by a woman indignantly questioning how we had the arrogance to make records for women when not every woman could make a record.

Another woman noted that there were African American women who had a lot of facial hair, and so our embracing a trans woman was doubly insulting to them. This drew lots of nods from the group.

Many women chimed in with the litany of horrors we were perpetrating by working with Sandy: polluting the lesbian feminist movement; denying engineering jobs to all the good engineers who were "real" women; invalidating the pain of "real" women who had never menstruated; reducing what it meant to be a lesbian to a set of surgically created genitals.

Many of these women were not strangers to us. We had worked with them, played with them, gotten high with them. Every now and then, one of them would pull a chair into the middle of the circle, climb onto it, and scream at us.

In the beginning, we tried to respond, to explain, to defend ourselves and Sandy. But it soon became clear that nobody was interested in what we had to say. They were angry and they wanted to yell at us. Period. Why we let them go on as long as we did is beyond me. I'm sure it was part of our attempt to be accountable to our community. I suppose we thought that eventually we would find some common ground, as we had, however briefly, with the Seattle Separatists. Maybe we were all just in shock that our so-called sisters could be saying these things to and about us. And, of course, we expected ourselves to tough things out, no matter how difficult. Whatever the reason, we stayed much too long. What finally got us out of the room was Jennifer, who went into the bathroom and became hysterical. She couldn't stop crying. She was shaking and moaning and dissociating. Jennifer was physically manifesting what all of us were feeling—she was dissolving in front of our eyes. I had never seen anything like this, and I was terrified. A friend came into the bathroom and gave us some Valium to give to Jennifer and told us to go home. We did.

Once we got home, Jennifer recovered quickly. But in a certain way, this day, which we forever after referred to as Slimy Sunday, changed us. This was a wound that never healed. If the intention of the women at the meeting was to convince us to change our minds about Sandy, they failed miserably. Instead, we became much more protective of her and more determined to stand by our decision to work with her. We became much more defensive generally, much less willing to open ourselves to the community, much more closed about our process. We felt battered and betrayed. We would continue to work with Sandy, continue to make records, even continue to hold on to our vision, but the vision was tainted now. I started to become cynical about the Women's Movement and about the lesbian community. I don't think I ever believed that we were all one big happy family, but even in spite of all the criticism that had come our way for one thing or another, I had not believed that lesbians could be so cruel to each other. My time of believing in magic was over.

The battle lines have been redrawn in the ensuing decades, but the battle still rages inside the feminist communities (to say nothing of how it rages outside). There are "sides": there are feminists who still call for boycotts of feminist institutions, businesses, and practitioners whose approach to, and degree of inclusion of, transgender people is different from their own. Women still throw accusations around like knives, and they still do deep damage. There are feminists who, while not calling for boycotts, still believe that trans women are not "real" women. These feminists support an end to discrimination against transgender people, but they do not believe trans women should be allowed to attend women-only events, or represent themselves as women. Then, there are feminists who believe strongly that no one who identifies as a woman should be excluded, and who staunchly resist linking femaleness to certain reproductive organs.

In spite of these strongly felt differences, I still had the idea that now there was enough *common* ground among those of us who have been around since the 1970s for us to be able to have a conversation. I discovered recently that a friend of mine was friends with one of the women who had been very vocal and very accusatory during Slimy Sunday. I asked my friend to ask her friend if she would be willing to speak with me—I made it very clear that I didn't want to argue with her. I wanted to listen to what she had to say about how it was for her then, whether she saw things differently now, whether there was any ground that we shared. My friend's friend declined. She wouldn't say why.

17 WOMANLY WAY

Making the Poetry Album

I WAS TOLD FROM A VERY young age that I was smart. I was already reading by the time I hit kindergarten (my Aunt Sally had taught me), so I skipped first grade. I was tracked with the college-bound kids and, in high school, was in all the Advanced Placement courses. But I didn't think of myself as smart. Sure, I got As in advanced algebra and biology; I knew history and could write pretty well. Grades were one thing, but sophisticated understanding was something else, and I was pretty sure I didn't have that.

Quite simply, I did not understand poetry, and, to me, that was the true test of intelligence. I didn't understand the metaphors, the symbols, the flowery language of what we were given to read and learn. What were these guys (and they were almost all guys) trying to say? It must have been very important, and I was just too shallow to get it. In my senior year in high school, in my small AP English class with a very select group of students and a notoriously no-bullshit teacher, we were given a homework assignment the first day—read "Trees" by Joyce Kilmer and be prepared to discuss it in class. "Trees" was a classic. We probably had read it every year since sixth grade, and every year we were taught that this was the standard for great poetry. Honestly, I didn't get what was great about it, but

I was sure that that was my problem. So when we got to class on day two and the teacher asked whether this was a good poem or not, I was prepared to talk about the brilliance of the language, the imagery, etc. Thank god she called on someone other than me—it was a boy named Steven, and he said, "This is a terrible poem." I was shocked. I was sure the teacher would throw him out of the class, or at least flunk him peremptorily. But no. She smiled at him and asked him to explain. Steven went on to talk about how Kilmer had mixed his metaphors and done other horrible things to the language. I couldn't even pay attention to everything he was saying because I was so shocked. When he was finished, the teacher validated all his points and thanked him.

But did I feel vindicated? No, I did not. I felt confused. If dozens of teachers and editors and anthologists thought this was so great, and it had just been shown to be a pretty pathetic piece of poetry, how was I supposed to know what was good and what wasn't? The safest course for me was to avoid all poetry at all costs. And so I did.

Until one day in early in 1971 when I opened up a copy of the DC feminist paper *off our backs* and I saw some poems by a woman named Judy Grahn. The set was called "The Common Woman Poems," and I paid them little notice until I got to the one titled "Carol, in the park, chewing on straws," and the first lines grabbed me by the heart:

> She has taken a woman lover
> whatever shall we do
> she has taken a woman lover
> how lucky it wasn't you

I kept reading.

And all the day through she smiles and lies
and grits her teeth and pretends to be shy,
or weak, or busy. Then she goes home
and pounds her own nails, makes her own
bets, and fixes her own car, with her friend.
She goes as far
as women can go without protection
from men.

This was *not* metaphor that made no sense, no flowery language
hiding the true meaning. This was poetry I understood. This
was my life. And although I myself had written extensively
and enthusiastically in *The Furies* about lesbianism, I had not
written about myself as a person. We did not talk about our daily
lives or how we got through our days when we were not in the
cocoon of our lesbian feminist collective and community. *The
Furies* was an instrument of the mind, intended to reach into
the minds of other women and convince them of the rightness
of our politics. What stunned me so much about Judy's poetry
was that she took language that was direct and rooted in reality
and made art of it. It had heart.

Judy came to DC in 1973, and Meg and I went to hear her
read "The Common Woman Poems" and more of her work. I
clearly remember sitting in the room watching her read and
being awestruck. She was so smart and powerful and dykey.
I thought I might have to change my attitude about poetry.
And one of my very first ideas as I thought about starting
this record company was that I wanted to record Judy Grahn
reading her poetry.

After the reading, Meg and I approached Judy and invited
her to our house for dinner. That night I was a nervous wreck—
one of my big fears has always been that I won't know what
to say, that I won't be able to carry on a conversation. And this

wasn't just anybody coming to dinner. This was a newfound hero. There was, however, one topic of conversation that I knew I could go to—Meg and I were going to ask her to record an album of her poetry with Olivia.

So, we did. Judy reacted as if it were no big deal, (although many years later she told me that she had been thrilled). However, she had a proviso before agreeing to a record. She told us that she had a deal with Pat Parker that if one of them were asked to do an album she would insist that the other be included. This was a first for me—an artist not asking for more but asking for less, giving up half of her record to another poet. We didn't know Pat's work, but I thought that we could figure that part out later; and if Judy thought she was good she probably was. She told us that Pat was a black lesbian poet who wrote with courage and beauty and enormous conviction about being black in a white world, being lesbian in a straight world, being working class in an affluent world, being a woman in a man's world. So we said "sure," and Judy said "sure." Later, in her memoir, *A Simple Revolution* (Aunt Lute, 2012), Judy said, "I was flattered, but just barely hiding my skepticism; lots of people had big ideas. Making them come true was the tricky part."

We didn't get to it as quickly as I had originally thought we would, but in 1976 we recorded LF 909—*Where Would I Be Without You: The Poetry of Pat Parker & Judy Grahn*. Each woman did a side. Their poems were fierce, loving, lesbian, sexy, political, and brilliantly read. We did the recording at Sandy Stone's house in Boulder Creek. This was a very simple recording that required no bells and whistles, and we thought that putting Pat and Judy in Sandy's living room would not only save us a ton of money over renting a studio, it would also give the poets a more comfortable space in which to record. I think I was touring with Meg during the recording, and I never made it to watch. But Sandy Stone said, "That was a religious experience, like being in the presence of masters of their craft."

Judy read from *Edward the Dyke and Other Poems* (The Women's Press Collective, 1971), *The Common Woman* (1974), and *She Who* (Diana Press, 1972). Pat read from *Child of Myself* (The Women's Press Collective, 1972), *Womanslaughter* (subsequently published by the The Women's Press Collective, 1978), and this from *Pit Stop* (The Women's Press Collective, 1975):

> My lover is a woman
> > & when I hold her -
> > > feel her warmth -
> > > I feel good - feel safe
>
> then/ I never think of
> > my families' voices -
> > never hear my sisters say -
> > bulldaggers, queers, funny -
> > come see us, but don't
> > bring your friends -
> > it's okay with us,
> > but don't tell mama
> > > it'd break her heart
> > never feel my father
> > turn in his grave
> > never hear my mother cry
> > Lord, what kind of child is this?
>
> > …
>
> My lover's hair is blonde
> > & when it rubs across my face
> > > it feels soft -
> > > feels like a thousand fingers

touch my skin & hold me
and i feel good.

...

And when we go to a gay bar
& my people shun me because i crossed
the line
& her people look to see what's
wrong with her - what defect
drove her to me -

And when we walk the streets
of this city - forget and touch
or hold hands and the people
stare, glare, frown, & taunt
at those queers -

I remember-
Every word taught me
Every word said to me
Every deed done to me
& then I hate -
i look at my lover
& for an instance - doubt -

Then/ i hold her hand tighter
And i can hear my mother cry.
Lord, what kind of child is this.

Judy was right about Pat, of course. Her writing was clear,
direct, and deliberately non-metaphorical. She believed that
the situation of black people in America required a language of
precision and power that must not be hinted at or inferred. Pat's
poetry was often more personal than Judy's, and she read with

a little more drama, which made the words really jump off the page, or, in this case, the vinyl. Both women were enormously pleased with the record, as were we.

We had no expectations that this would be a big seller, and we were right about that, but by the middle of 1977, we had sold 2,400 copies, which was enough to recoup our costs of $7,000. Thankfully, sales figures are not the only means by which we judge success. In their introduction to *The Journal of Lesbian Studies* (June 15, 2015), Cheryl Clarke and Julie R. Enszer wrote:

> Forty years after the release of *Where Would I Be Without You*, a generation of young people do not know what record albums are. Phonographs, album covers, A side and B side, record sleeves, and liner notes are things from the past. In an age when music is most often received in a digital form, the work of Pat Parker and Judy Grahn continues to be resonant for a new generation of lesbians and feminists.
>
> ...
>
> Judy Grahn and Pat Parker were integral to how we lesbians imagined our voices in the world. They gave us voice. In 1973, in "The Common Women Poems," [*sic*] Grahn wrote, "the common woman is as common / as the common crow…as the reddest wine…as a thunderstorm…. as a nail…" She told us lesbians that we could take up the stories of ordinary women of extraordinary courage. Grahn and Parker asserted a "dyke" identity for all to adopt, an identity integrally shaped by a desire for sex and a desire for freedom.

Pat died in 1989, but her poetry is still read because it is still absolutely relevant. Thankfully, Judy Grahn is still very much alive, still writing, and still impacting people all over the world. Her poems have been translated and published in Spain, Denmark, Germany, and probably other countries as well. She is a master of language, and has used her writing as a way to reclaim words and signs of lesbian culture that are meant to be derogatory—dyke, bulldyke, bulldagger. She has written a novel, a memoir, cultural histories, dramas, essays, and more poetry. Although she can, intentionally, get very erudite and abstract, most of her writing is grounded in language and meaning that goes right to my core. She still takes my breath away.

For me, more than anything—other than Meg's *I Know You Know*—*Where Would I Be Without You* was a project of my heart. This record represented the essence of why I wanted to start a women's record company in the first place. As Judy said about women's poetry, from "Anathema," which we printed on the back of the album jacket:

> art is not a way out, there is no way out.
> there is only what we've got and how to turn it
> around to reinforce our fighting genius; to
> clarify and point out what has been stolen
> from us and that we must take it back or continue
>   with nothing.
> at its best it comes from our bitterest anger,
> our most expansive love, our most courageous
> hopes, our most vital visions, our most honest
> insights, our fiercest determination.

18 DON'T PRAY FOR ME

**Homophobia and
Lesbian Concentrate**

THIS IS WHAT IT WAS like to be gay in the 1970s in most of
America, even eight years after Stonewall—the insurrection
that marked the beginning of the gay civil rights movement in the US. If you were lesbian or gay, to your landlord
you referred to your lover as your roommate or your friend or
he could evict you, if he had even consented to rent to you in
the first place. If your employer found out, you could be fired.
Your parents or your husband could have you committed to a
mental institution, and, until 1973, homosexuality was considered a mental illness and was included in the Diagnostic and
Statistical Manual of Mental Disorders created by the American
Psychiatric Association. In a custody battle, you were sure to
lose your children to your ex-husband—no matter what kind
of derelict or degenerate he was—as long as he wasn't gay too.
It was assumed that you were a sexual predator who enjoyed
having sex with children. You did not hold your lover's hand in
public, and you certainly didn't kiss her or show any other kind
of affection publicly. If you subscribed to gay periodicals, you
made sure they were delivered to you in a plain brown wrapper.
The Left accused you of indulging in bourgeois individualism
that would hurt the cause. Parts of the Women's Movement
accused you of introducing a lavender herring into their agenda

and hurting the cause. Some men, including policemen, thought it was their prerogative to rape lesbians to punish them for daring to prefer women to men. Others thought all a lesbian needed was a good screwing by a manly man, and she would come over to their side. There was so much more. Many of these things are still happening.

In spite of all this, people kept coming out, writing and publishing books, performing music and comedy in concerts and on records, opening coffee houses and bookstores, health clinics and community centers. There were music festivals and legal defense funds, print collectives and land trusts. And there were myriad ways to find and connect with each other: newsletters, call centers, and lesbian rap groups.

Eventually, some cities began passing anti-discrimination ordinances. Miami, Florida, was one of the first. On January 18, 1977, the Dade County Commission approved a law that would outlaw discrimination on the basis of sexual orientation in employment, housing, and public services. It was thanks to effective lobbying by a new organization called the Dade County Coalition for the Humanistic Rights of Gays. Not surprisingly, local churches began denouncing the ordinance from the pulpit and organizing against it. Emerging from among all the opposition figures was a 36-year-old former Miss Oklahoma, born-again Christian, and paid spokesperson for the Florida Citrus Commission. Her name was Anita Bryant. They named their campaign Save Our Children.

Bryant became the face and the voice of a virulently homophobic campaign that spread around the country to repeal and/or defeat any and all local anti-discrimination laws. The Wikipedia entry says,

> The Save Our Children campaign produced a local television commercial showing the "wholesome

entertainment" of the Orange Bowl Parade (which Bryant hosted), contrasting that with highly sexualized images of the San Francisco Gay Freedom Day Parade, including men in leather harnesses kissing each other, dancing drag queens, and topless women. The commercial's announcer accused Miami's gay community of trying to turn Miami into the "hotbed of homosexuality" that San Francisco had become. Full-page newspaper ads were run in *The Miami Herald*, with made-up headlines claiming teachers were having sex with their students, children were being lured into prostitution rings, and homosexuals were insinuating themselves into youth organizations, followed by the question "Are all homosexuals nice? …There is no 'human right' to corrupt our children."

For the most part, none of the attacks even acknowledged the existence of lesbians. We were, after all, just women, and besides, nobody could figure out what lesbians did in bed—how was it possible to have sex without having a penis involved? Regardless, we understood that we would not be exempt from the results of these campaigns. We knew we had to act: we just didn't know how. And then, over lunch one day in the Olivia house during a discussion of Bryant's latest outrage, Jennifer said, "Well, we're a record company. We should make a record."

We were in the middle of producing Meg's second album (*Face the Music*, LF 913) and we had plans for the rest of 1977 and 1978 with albums by Linda Tillery, Gwen Avery, Mary Watkins and another by Cris Williamson. We had no budget for an additional album, to say nothing of time. But this was one of those "stop the presses" moments. Once Jennifer said it, we all knew that making a record in response to the ugly campaign that Anita Bryant was leading was our best response. It was as if Olivia had been created for just this moment.

We decided on an anthology—a Lesbianthology—of music and poetry. We used some material that we had already recorded and released on other albums, like Meg's *Ode to a Gym Teacher*, Cris's *Sweet Woman*, *Kahlua Mama* from BeBe K'Roche, Teresa Trull's *Woman-Loving Women*, and poems from Pat Parker—*For Straight Folks Who Don't Mind Gays But Wish They Weren't So Blatant*—and Judy Grahn—*A History of Lesbianism*. We got permission from the Berkeley Women's Music Collective to use a song from their album, *Gay and Proud*. All the others would be newly recorded, either in the studio we were already using for Meg's new album, or in what we were jokingly calling "Olivia Records' Studio A," also known as 739 Gramercy Drive, the living room of the original Olivia house where Teresa, Jennifer, and Judy lived.

Sandy Stone had begun building a 16-channel modular console, which she saw as the first piece of equipment for our own studio, and this was her opportunity to try it out. We rented a piano and put that in the living room as well.

Mary Watkins came in with two new songs, both written in response to Anita Bryant. The first was "Don't Pray for Me" and Linda Tillery sang the lead.

> I know why you cry Sister Nita
> Life's passin' you by while rules enslave you
> And it's your blind innocence that traps you
> That makes you think it's the wrong I do
>
> ...
>
> Don't pray for me proper lady
> Pray for the truth your money can't buy

Don't pray for me bitter woman
The happy slave is a lie

…

So don't take pride in your innocence
It won't make you pure and holy
Stop quotin' scriptures out of context
To stir up fear and bigotry
You needn't worry 'bout my soul 'Nita
You need the time to heal your own
We're comin' out to walk in the sunlight
We're comin' out to fight for right.

Mary's second song, on which she sang lead, was a love song of sorts to a friend who was afraid to come out, called "No Hidin' Place."

My sweet sister
Let my heart tell you how
I know your fear
Of losing all that's dear
But trust your heart
Trust your heart to let you know
And to recognize a choice
Or the sound of your own voice

…

Sweet woman
Sweet sister
Something new
And good has happened to you
Let it shine, let it shine, let it shine
Love is not a shame

> Let it be your claim
> Let it be, let it be, let it be!
>
> …
>
> There's no hidin' place
> No hidin' place
> No hidin' place over there.

Gwen Avery recorded "Sugar Mama" in the living room. Sandy got a live recording of Meg singing "Nina" in concert, a song she had co-written with Holly. Sue Fink went into the studio and recorded the song she co-wrote with Joelyn Grippo.

> Here come the lesbians
> Here come the leaping lesbians
>
> …
>
> Don't go and try to fight it
> Run away or try to hide it
> We want your love and that's our plan
> Here come the lesbians

Teresa found a song by Gertrude "Ma" Rainey, "Prove It on Me Blues":

> They say I do it, ain't nobody caught me
> They sure gotta prove it on me
>
> …
>
> I went out last night with a crowd of my friends
> They must've been women, 'cause I don't like no men
> It's true I wear a collar and a tie,
> I like to watch the women as they pass by

On June 7, 1977, the citizens of Dade County voted over-whelmingly to repeal the gay rights ordinance. Bryant allegedly danced a jig when the results were announced and told reporters, "All America and all the world will hear what the people have said, and with God's continued help, we will prevail in our fight to repeal similar laws throughout the nation which attempt to legitimize a life style that is both perverse and dangerous." Now that lesbians and gay men can marry, serve openly in the military, adopt children, and so much more, I assume that Anita knows that God switched sides.

In spite of, or maybe because of, the electoral defeat, we did not slow down. We decided to donate part of the album proceeds to the Lesbian Mothers' National Defense Fund and include information about them in the album insert. We also started compiling a list of "woman-produced recordings of interest to lesbians," women's publishing houses, and almost one hundred lesbian/feminist community organizations around the US, all of which we included in the album insert.

In a report for a collective meeting on June 28, 1977, I wrote:

> [I]n addition to mechanicals [songwriting royalties] which everyone gets 2-cents-a-record-sold (except Pat, Judy and Ma Rainey), we would pay performers: Cris—5 cents; Sue Fink—5 cents; BeBe K'Roche—3 cents each; Gwen—5 cents; Pat—7 cents; Judy—7 cents; Berkeley Women's Music Collective—16 cents total. Meg, Teresa, Mary and Tui [Linda Tillery] lovingly donate their services. Lesbian Mothers get 10 cents on the first 5000 sold and 25 cents forever after. Everything seems to be proceeding apace. Distributors have been contacted about providing us with store names for inclusion on the ads. Ads will be traded with papers in exchange for records which papers can use for their own promo

giveaways. Total budget for the first 5000 is around $13,000 including high estimates of everything. Price is $5.50 before September 1 and $6.00 after.

We finished recording in early July and sent the tapes off to be mastered and to get a test pressing. By this time, we knew the album would be called *Lesbian Concentrate*, and it was Kate's idea to put an orange juice can on the cover.

The simple-yet-iconic album cover

We printed up stickers with the orange juice can and "Silent No More!" in big, bold letters. We took them with us everywhere we went. A couple of us went to the very sterile and homophobic

Disneyland and plastered our Lesbian Concentrate stickers on rides, restaurants, and restrooms.

Liza Williams, our newly hired publicity and promotion person, thought we might get some mainstream media coverage for the album, which put me in a bit of a bind. I was not yet out to my parents. I would only see them once or twice a year at most—they were in Connecticut, on the other side of the country. When I did see them, we would have heated arguments about politics, which started when I tried to convince them to stop supporting the war in Vietnam. My father told me I should go live in Russia if I didn't like it here, and after that I stopped trying. I told them as little about my life as possible, although they knew I had started a record company, and once, when Meg had a concert in Hartford, we both stayed at their house. Separate bedrooms, of course. I certainly didn't want them to discover their middle daughter was a lesbian by reading it in *Time Magazine*. And then, too, I thought it was hypocritical of me to urge women to come out while I was still hidden from my parents. I talked to my younger sister, who lived near the parents, about what she thought would be the best way to tell them. She decided, without consulting me, that the best way would be for her to tell them herself, which she did. My father said nothing. My mother said "I'm going to throw up." But she didn't. They survived and eventually came to like the woman I've been with for the past twenty-four years.

The album came out in August 1977, and it was an immediate hit by our standards, selling almost 7,500 copies before the end of the year. There was criticism from the usual sources (not political enough, too late to the party, etc.), but there was also praise from women we hadn't heard much from before—women who identified as gay, whose community was in the bars, who didn't think of themselves as feminists. We cut a 45 with two songs from all our albums (the exception being the poetry album), not to sell but to get them on jukeboxes in lesbian bars. We had minimal success with that, but for Lesbian Concentrate we cut a 45 with Gwen's "Sugar Mama" on the A side and Teresa's "Woman-Loving Women" on the B. Distributors had no trouble getting this into the bars, and "Sugar Mama" in particular was getting a lot of play.

We had great joy in making this album. It was certainly not the most coherent musically, and the performances were uneven. But this was one case where we let our politics override our aesthetics. We were angry, we were fired up, and we were strategic. We thought that many women would look to us for a response, and we wanted our statement to be big, bold, brazenly lesbian, and with a clear and strong declaration of our politics. There was nothing subtle or nuanced or delicate about any part of it. We made a record that was a loud, proud explosion of lesbianism—forty-seven minutes of unbridled lesbian joy.

And to nail it home, in case anyone had any doubts, Robin and I wrote a lengthy statement for the album insert, titled "Out to change the world!" which said, in part:

> What is a lesbian? A lesbian is a woman who loves women, who counts on women for her emotional support, who looks to women for her growth, who finds her identity in her womanhood. A lesbian is a woman who, more and more willingly, and with more and more pride, knows and shows her own strength, makes her own definitions for herself, and dares to defy society's most sacred taboo—"Thou shalt not live without men and like it."
>
> ....
>
> Lesbians threaten this society because we threaten men. People who have power are afraid of those things they can't control. A woman who refuses to be

a submissive partner to a man, a woman who refuses to act in male-defined "feminine" ways, a woman who has her own strength and is not dependent on a man's being "good" to her for her support, a woman who recognizes the experiences and feelings she shares with other women, a woman who feels the bonds she has with other women—such a woman will not put up with male dominance and the male abuse of power, as is expected of women. Such a woman will say yes to her own strength and yes to her own liberation. And in this society, that will not do.

....

For lesbians now, this is a time of great challenge and great potential. We must remember that the differences we have among ourselves are miniscule in comparison with the differences we have with our true enemies—the people who hold power over us and make our lives difficult. We have survived throughout history under conditions even worse than the ones we now live in. We have something now that lesbians have never had before—we have each other, out front, publicly proclaiming our strength, our love, our pride in ourselves, and our joy at being woman-loving women. Let us always celebrate ourselves, and let us make each celebration a new step towards our liberation.

19 WILD THINGS

Radical Feminism and Advanced Capitalism

N RETROSPECT, SO MUCH OF our strategy was ridiculous on its face. We wanted to get past the defenses and into the hearts of straight women everywhere. We believed, at least for a while, that if they could just hear the music, they would leave their men, march in the streets, and stand with us as we overthrew the patriarchy. So we tried, with great seriousness of purpose, to gain access to and attention from radio stations, record stores, top-notch nightclubs, and taste-making music reviewers. At the same time, we were openly contemptuous of the radio stations, record stores, top-notch nightclubs, and taste-making music reviewers and were doing everything we could think of to render them powerless and irrelevant by building up alternative feminist institutions wherever we could. It is no surprise that we didn't accomplish these goals and that we drove ourselves a little crazy in the attempt.

This chapter could be called by one of two aphorisms we invented and liked to bandy about:

- Process is our most important product (this came to me from an ad for General Electric, which said "progress is our most important product"); or

- Struggle is hard. That's why we don't call it fiesta. (This was Jennifer's.)

Between March 1975, when we arrived in Los Angeles, and October 1977, when we moved to the Bay Area, we recorded six albums, released seven—*I Know You Know, The Changer and the Changed, BeBe K'Roche, Where Would I Be Without You, The Ways a Woman Can Be* (Teresa Trull), *Lesbian Concentrate*, and *Face the Music* (Meg's second album)—and were in production on an eighth (*Linda Tillery*). We had published songbooks for *I Know You Know* and *Changer*. We were distributing albums by Kay Gardner, the Berkeley Women's Music Collective, Joanna Cazden, and Casse Culver. Our artists were touring pretty constantly, and we were booking the tours, road-managing, and usually conducting post-concert workshops. Our distribution network had grown to over sixty women and they were selling records in big and medium-sized cities and small towns all across the US and Puerto Rico. We were in New York and Pocatello; Albuquerque and Vermillion; South Dakota, Chicago, and Chico; and lots of places in between. Needless to say, our original group of five (Jennifer, Kate, Judy, Meg, me) had grown. But our principles of working non-hierarchically, making decisions collectively, and valuing all work equally remained in place.

In a never-ending quest to find the perfect structure, we had created a living collective that was separate from the working collective, added women to the working collective and brought in women who wanted to work with us but didn't want to be in the collective. The original five still constituted a living collective in which we shared whatever income we had as well as our cars and other big-ticket items, and we all took the same draw. When new women started working with us, they were offered the option to join the living collective—some declined and some accepted. When Teresa arrived—a white, working-class woman from North Carolina—she immediately joined the living collective, and, to her, it represented her first experience of financial security. The collective paid our rent, food, medical bills, gas, and cars, and, at one point in the fall of 1976, our personal draw increased to $15 a week. Teresa thought this made us all equal, until she noticed that some of the middle-class women were getting large gifts from their families—she remembered one of us getting a color TV. We might all use these things, but they belonged to only one person. We spent a lot of time trying to figure out how to make things equitable and not just equal. We didn't just want everyone to have the same things as everyone else; we wanted everyone to get what she needed, and that meant some would have more than others.

We were in the middle of a huge growth spurt on every level, which was thrilling and terrifying as we tried to navigate our way through advanced capitalism, systemic racism, misogyny, homophobia, and centuries of patriarchy while following a feminist path. Not exactly a piece of cake.

We processed endlessly, and we struggled about everything. It was extremely important to us that we make the right decisions. It wasn't just that we were under intense scrutiny from about half the lesbians and feminists in the country, many of whom were waiting for us to screw up. We also believed. We believed that every decision, every action, every word out of our mouths should reflect our values. But what to do when we had conflicting values?

Process, process, process. Struggle, struggle, struggle.

We had a lot more meetings, and there were a lot more voices. We had been deliberate about how we were expanding, so the women of Olivia now included black women, white working-class women, women even younger than us, a couple of straight women, a trans woman, and one older woman.

We met and began working with Liza Williams, who was straight and in her fifties at the time. (We thought she was very old.) Liza had worked for many years at Island and Capitol Records and had done promotion for Pink Floyd, a British rock band who got famous in the late '60s. There are stories now on the Internet that she was the girlfriend of the poet Charles Bukowski for a while, but she never discussed this with us. She had apparently been fired from her last major label job. She needed work and was at least a little interested in what we were doing.

Unfortunately, Liza had bipolar disorder and occasionally stopped taking her medication; she needed a lot of attention and we gave it to her. She knew things that we didn't know. She knew how to write copy for album jackets and press releases that didn't sound like our style, which was a cross between Mao's *Little Red Book* and the TV show *Dragnet*—just the facts, ma'am. An example of her copy from Teresa Trull's album *The Ways a Woman Can Be*:

> Growing out of the green and glowing vegetation of North Carolina with her guitar growing out of her arm and a song in her head as well as her heart (which is the difference between songs that say 'oh baby oh' and *The Ways a Woman Can Be)*, Teresa at sixteen was a working musician. She paid for groceries by singing with a band obsessed with rock and roll while the blues kept her secretly sane.

Just having someone on our staff whose job was promotion was hard for me to handle. Everything about it seemed so dishonest and manipulative to me. What would come next? How far was the distance between selling and selling out? I worried about this constantly. We had hired Liza, asked her to promote our records and our artists, and then resisted—at least initially—almost everything she wanted to do. But we knew we had to do something different if we were going to have the kind of impact we wanted.

We did not want the musicians we recorded and produced to be thought of or treated like "stars." The musicians had control of their music and their records, but they got paid on the same basis as everyone else. For many years, Meg would not sign autographs until she finally got tired of explaining why her signature was not more valuable than the person asking for it and gave in. We did not want to glorify the musicians. At the same time, we understood that selling records was how we planned to finance the revolution, and it was the musicians who sold the records.

At the end of December 1976, as we were readying Teresa's album for release, we spent two days in meetings trying to come up with a policy on using the images of the featured musician. From my notes on the first day of meetings:

> Long discussion followed about images, promotion, star-trips, etc., or in other words, the promo committee idea of the Teresa poster, which was a 17″ x 23″ poster with a full picture of Teresa raised an eyebrow here and there about whether it was star-trippy. Points were raised about whether whole concept of putting one woman on album cover is star-trippy. Questions raised about whether nature of photo, nature of performer is what makes a difference—i.e. the actual photo of Teresa that's going on the album cover was generally agreed to be not a star-trippy photo, so is putting it on the poster by itself (without the actual cover) just another degree of the same thing or is it actually promoting Teresa and not the album? How much do our album covers reflect our politics anyway? How much can they and still be useful

in selling records? We all got hysterical as the meeting lasted 3 hours so we decided to meet again tomorrow.

Jennifer reported on the second meeting:

> Liza says it's not necessary to sale of records to have artists' picture on the front—that, in fact, if we're promoting the music and not the person, it'd be better to use other art. Points out that it's a good way to make women's art accessible additionally. Says particularly irrelevant to use artist image on first album of little known artist. Mary [Watkins] points out that it is this person who's representing the message we're trying to get out and that we have no control over who's going to star-trip Teresa. Judy feels that a main point is that the picture is not star-trippy and offers a strong image, that it is very attractive and will help sell albums. Kate talks about objectification. That regardless of how the picture is, repeated use eventually makes it a caricature of the person. After a long and painful discussion, we are unable to make a policy. Feel that each case must be individually considered in light of what it conveys graphically.
>
> Consensus, however, that the connection between this picture and the title *The Ways a Woman Can Be* is at best tenuous and that the title has more potential than that. Kate and Teresa will work on a better cover.

A few days later, Judy, not satisfied with our decision, sent a letter to everyone:

> When I look at that picture as it sits in front of me I see a very wonderful image. It's a terribly warm, loving picture that would say to any straight woman looking at it…it's safe for me to listen to this.

In a world where album covers have become totally disgusting images of women being raped or liking being sex objects, a photo like this is an incredible contrast. The image is not all the alternatives but at least it is expressing one that never gets seen. This is not your typical woman identity on album covers.

I do not see a star in this picture...I see regular and that's who Teresa is so it's okay with me...

Judy's argument won the day. This is the image
that caused us so much consternation.

The great irony here is that, for Teresa Trull, the unknown artist, we used the artist's picture on the front. For Linda

Tillery's, we used women's art. That was Linda's choice. Linda was well known to R&B lovers, especially in the Bay Area, having put out a couple of albums with mainstream labels RCA and CBS, and it would have been easier to promote the album if people had seen her face on the cover. Instead, her picture appeared on the back.

There were lots more promotional questions that had us pulling our hair out. We released *Linda Tillery* on December 1, 1977. Leopold's, the great independent record store on Telegraph Avenue in Berkeley, reported that sales were brisk and that they were seeing lots of black women come into the store to buy the record. Leopold's wanted to set up a big in-store display and they thought they could sell a lot more if we would partner with them on some ads. In particular, they wanted to buy time on KRE, a local R&B radio station with a large black listenership. KRE was already playing the album, and we understood that there would likely be even more airplay if we advertised. What could we have possibly found to object to?

My concern was that we would be sending customers to Leopold's, and not to the women's bookstores. Of course we hoped that Linda's album would reach a new audience that didn't know Olivia Records or Women's Music, and that this would be their portal to lesbian feminism. We also knew that it was the women's bookstores that gave us shelf space and sold our concert tickets and played our albums all day long in the store and were built on principles much closer to ours than Leopold's. We didn't have to spend two days deciding to do the ads with Leopold's, but it was another example of the way we struggled with every decision, the way we insisted on looking at every side of every issue and understanding the choices we were making and the consequences.

One more story. We were producing concerts in Oakland and Berkeley in halls that sat anywhere from 2,000 to 3,400 people and selling out all or almost all the seats. We sold all our tickets as general admission—no reserved seating. So when we opened the doors, hundreds of women (and a few men) made a mad dash for the best seats. I wanted us to consider selling reserved tickets. I wrote this in a 1978 memo to the collective:

> Reserved tickets (seating) at concerts. The main advantage of this is the avoidance of stampede when the doors open for general admission concerts; that people don't have to come 3 hours early to stand in line to get good seats, etc. The disadvantage is that she who has money early gets a better seat than she who has money late. There are several ways to do it if we want to. One is to charge one ticket price but just sell reserved seats.... Another way is to charge different prices for tickets and have the prices all mixed up—I mean the most expensive seats would not all be in the front and the cheapest seats would not all be in the back. However, probably then someone who was buying a ticket late would end up paying more money for not such a good seat. Third alternative is to have the best seats be the most expensive, etc. This is a drag.

The decision on this day was to continue to sell all seats as general admission, although eventually we did change to reserved seating. But we tried to put every action and decision through a feminist lens—for us, that automatically meant considering race and class. Under these circumstances, it's astonishing to see how much we accomplished. Processing everything collectively was exhausting, but it was also exhilarating because we were actively and consciously living out our values in a community of women.

While some of the struggles we engaged in may seem trivial, it's important to remember that we engaged in these struggles because we honestly believed that we were creating the world we wanted to live in. We never took our eyes off the prize. The prize was not sold-out concert halls or gold records, although we would have loved having that. The prize was not having more Women's Music being produced and recorded by all-female crews and bands, nor was it having women and lesbians running corporations, serving in the military, being able to get credit cards, getting equal pay, keeping their children in custody battles, ending rape and all forms of violence against women—some of which we actively worked for, and all of which we supported. The prize was a complete upending of the system that used political and economic power to divide people from each other, by gender, race, class, sexuality, physical and mental ability, nationality, religion—that kept us fighting each other over one tiny piece of pie, instead of working together to bake a whole new pie. The prize was a world based on "power to" rather than power over. The prize was a world where everyone had enough, and survival was not an issue. The prize was seeing everyone able to fulfill whatever their creative dreams were. The prize was not more money, more power over, more acquisition, more destruction. The prize was a world where our common values were justice, and peace, and equity. We thought all of that was worth struggling for.

We rarely thought about the financial implications of our choices. We did not want to be ruled or even influenced by considerations of money. But we ended up spending a huge amount of time and energy dealing with money, or rather, our lack of it. At the end of 1976, with three albums of our own and several others that we were distributing, and eight collective members who needed to live, we had $6,216.21 in our checking account and $5,183.47 in savings. Eventually, we were going to have to face the music about money.

20 SCARS

Race Matters

I T WAS ALWAYS OUR INTENTION to bring women of color into the Olivia collective. We wanted to expand the collective, and we wanted to expand the Women's Movement. In our minds, we could not call ourselves "feminists" if we were not including women from all races and classes in all the layers of our work. To just record a few women of color would not only be insufficient, it would have replicated the mainstream record industry which treated almost all their artists as money-making machines not fit to sit at the tables of power. Black artists in particular had a history of being ripped off and grossly mistreated by the labels.

We had brought two white, working-class women—Sandy Ramsey and Teresa Trull—into the collective, but that was relatively easy. At least some of us had lived with, studied with, worked with, and/or played with working-class women. Jennifer and I had done deep work in The Furies to understand and address class privilege, and now, in Olivia, all of us continued that work. Through many struggles and discussions in lengthy meetings we had developed, at least to some extent, a class consciousness and a class analysis. We had looked at the ways we operated as a middle-class organization and had implemented some practices to address our different degrees of class privilege. We made mistakes, but in general we felt that we had made a smooth transition bringing in Sandy and Teresa, and that they added a lot to Olivia's operations.

We knew how to talk about class. But we didn't know how to talk about race.

If today you were to Google "why is it so hard to talk about race," you would find hundreds of entries, but in 1976 those conversations were just beginning. We did know a few things. We knew that when we invited women of color to join us, we would not do it one at a time; there had to be at least two coming in at the same time, and more would be better. We thought they would need support from each other, and we also wanted the variety of wisdom and experience that each woman would bring. We didn't want to depend on one or two women of color to represent what all women of color thought or felt about anything, or to make them be responsible for widening our view. We knew that we would not be inviting them to assimilate into the Olivia as it then was—we expected that the culture of Olivia would change, and we had no idea what that meant. We knew that our comfortable ways of being with each other would be challenged and possibly changed. We knew that we did not want anything we did or said to be considered or called "racist." There was so much more that we did not know. What we did know was that there would be struggle for all of us, and that we were as ready as we could be to engage. And we knew that this had to be the way forward.

By the time we finished recording *BeBe K'Roche* in 1976, we had invited Linda Tillery to be part of the collective, and she had accepted. We were thrilled. Linda had options. She had been the lead singer with The Loading Zone, a Bay Area rock band that recorded for the RCA label in 1967. In 1970, Al Kooper of Blood, Sweat & Tears produced her first solo album on CBS, called *Sweet Linda Divine*. Neither album sold particularly well, but her amazing vocal abilities caught the attention of critics and people in the industry. She was offered a management deal with an industry insider that could have been her ticket to the big time. But there were two problems. The prospective manager wanted a 60/40 split on all earnings, with Linda getting the short end. This, she felt, smacked too much of how Black artists had been ripped off by white managers and record companies. And then there was the fact that she was a lesbian, and she feared that she would have to stay closeted if she went totally mainstream. Her experience working with Olivia on the BeBe K'Roche album was so positive for her that she decided to throw in with us.

Because she was taking care of her elderly mother in Oakland, moving to LA was not an option for her. We were not thrilled about LA ourselves—it was such an "industry" town, so hard for a small, alternative, women's record company to be noticed by the mainstream media and the clubs. We now had good connections with the pressing plant, the mastering labs, and the other industry outfits that we needed. LA had a vibrant women's culture, but the San Francisco Bay Area had that and more. Things seemed looser and more open to "alternatives." Plus, although she was spending a lot of time with us in LA, Linda lived in Oakland. The only downsides we could think of about living in the Bay Area were the necessity of moving and finding an office and space for all of us to live and the fear of earthquakes. We moved the whole operation to Oakland in October 1977.

While we were still in LA, Linda introduced us to her friend Michelle Clinton, an African American poet, and Michelle started working with us. Like all new coworkers, she started in packing and shipping, but she soon moved into our production department, where she learned to book tours for our artists and assist me in our ongoing Oakland-based concert series. She was anxious to learn more about the financial aspects of running a business, and we sent her, along with Jennifer and Liz Brown, an ex-distributor we had recently hired, to the New School for Democratic Management in San Francisco for a multi-week training class where they studied best practices in business and marketing.

We met Mary Watkins through Holly Near. Holly's piano accompanists had always been men, but now that she was identifying as a lesbian and touring with Meg, she wanted a female accompanist, and she found Mary through an ad. Mary had recently graduated *cum laude* with a Bachelor of Music degree from Howard University in Washington, DC. She was a brilliant composer and arranger, and she could play any and every style of music. She leaned heavily into jazz and classical, but she had no trouble working with Holly's pop and folk songs.

Soon after Mary started performing with Holly, Teresa Trull began planning for her album, which Linda Tillery would produce, and they needed a pianist. Mary was invited to audition. It took Teresa and Linda about one minute to hire her.

Mary was not overtly political in the ways that Linda and Michelle and the other Olives were, but she was a lesbian with a deep understanding of the meaning of oppression and liberation. She later told me that she didn't really understand what we meant by "Lesbian Feminism"; she was not used to so much heavy conversation about class and race and collectivity. But she had come to LA looking for a community, and she said "Olivia offered me the world—a community of women organized around music, and that's what I wanted." By the summer of 1977, Mary, Linda, and Michelle were part of the Olivia collective, and everyone was getting ready for the move north.

With the additions of Liz Brown and another white woman ex-distributor, Robin Brooks, we had now grown to fourteen women in the working collective. Seven of us were also in the living collective (Meg, Jennifer, Kate, Liz, Teresa, Judy, and me). We hired a couple of women to do particular jobs, especially around touring. They were not in the collective, but they participated in meetings where the topics impacted their work.

Figuring out how to pay everyone was, to say the least, a challenge. We had "employees," one Olivia collective member who owned property for which she "needed" money to maintain, collective members who came from some class privilege, and others who barely had a pot to pee in. And, to complicate matters, Olivia was not rolling in money. Once again, we struggled over how to define need, how to know what was enough, and for whom.

We had four working musicians on staff who were touring all the time, as well as writing, practicing, and recording their own music, working on someone else's album, or acting as the Olivia A&R (Artists & Repertoire) Department, which meant listening to the dozens of tapes we were receiving. They also were regular participants in all our business and political meetings. Because Meg and Teresa were in the living collective, their concert earnings went into the living collective pot. Linda and Mary were not part of the living collective, and they took jobs that Olivia booked and produced as well as jobs that we didn't. We had to figure out how to pay everyone fairly. When Mary, for example, was on the road with Holly, she wasn't doing Olivia work. She was being paid by Holly. Should she also draw her Olivia salary? Or were any of us really not always doing Olivia work?

Throw in an additional wrinkle because Linda was taking care of and helping to financially support her mother, and Mary had a teenage daughter. Linda and Mary were the only ones of us with dependents, and we all understood that to be able to work at Olivia Records, these women had to be able to take care of their families. We always operated close to the bone, but we made sure that everyone could pay their bills and have a little extra. Still, Mary has subsequently told me that she never felt financially secure during that time. I think now that Mary had a more realistic view of Olivia's finances than I did, certainly, and less of that middle-class confidence that money would always come from somewhere.

For yet another twist, Liza Williams, our marketing and promotion expert, was twenty to twenty-five years older than the rest of us. Liza wanted extra money because she was anticipating getting older and retiring. At the time, this seemed like a luxury to me and certainly beyond our capacity. We decided we could not accommodate that need then. Maybe later.

We constantly tried to figure out an equitable system. For example, at any given time, several Olives were collecting unemployment benefits, while others were being paid a salary. The salaried women filed tax returns and inevitably got refunds because the salaries were so low. The folks collecting unemployment did not. But we were all working for more or less the same amount of money, with exceptions for the women with dependents. So we agreed that the tax refunds didn't really belong to the salaried women and would be divided among all the collective members.

Our decisions about how to pay ourselves evolved over time. In the end, we agreed that we would all draw the same base pay; that women with dependents (Linda and Mary) would draw more; that Olivia musicians doing Olivia-produced concerts would not be paid extra for those concerts, but that anything they earned from non-Olivia-produced concerts, studio work, or touring was theirs to keep; and that the musicians would keep any songwriting royalties they were owed (although when money got tight, we put off making these payments until we could more easily afford them).

≈

Talking about money was always complicated, but not nearly as difficult as talking about race. There was an internal layer: how we made decisions, how we talked to each other, what we asked from each other—in other words, how race shaped the way we operated as a collective. There was an external layer: who we recorded and how we promoted them and how we talked about race in, and to, women's communities. Of course, these layers overlapped. These were some of the most challenging and demanding conversations we had.

For example, late in the summer of 1977, while Meg was finishing up her second album, *Face the Music,* Linda and Michelle asked for a meeting to discuss an issue that was bothering them. We gathered in the living room of one of the Olivia houses, pulling chairs in from everywhere and practically sitting on top of each other. The issue was a song that Meg had written and recorded for her new album. As Linda and Michelle spoke, it was impossible not to watch Meg's reaction. Meg was very newly sober, so she was feeling particularly vulnerable—she had no alcoholic fog to protect her.

The song was called "Rosalind." She described it as "a story about the time when I first began to understand the subtle and complex ways that racism works through me." Some of the lyrics:

> Oh Rosalind was my first black friend
> In '66 in North Carolina
> And we were twenty, in summer school
> When I heard her laughin' down the hall
> Such a fine laugh, so husky and hearty a laugh, I just
>   came running
>
> Well we found that we had lots in common
> Like music, drinking, and talking dirty
> Warbling, chortling until dawn

Self-conscious friends, but sincere
Making bad jokes about suntan and natural rhythm
   that we thought we'd invented!

   ....

(But in the corners of our hearts and our minds
I know we kept a tally of the telltale signs
That showed that though my intentions seemed fine
I was still my friend's oppressor)

And under the very white Southern blaze
She told me of the boys she'd loved
And though she teased and teased and teased
I told her nothing

(Ros and I had never touched, really
But then I never touched anyone, really…)

Then came our final day, in the rich red
   August afternoon
And there we were, just standing in my room,
   writhing in the silence apart

Then suddenly we ran into each other's arms
Swaying, swooning in the fierce tenderness of
   the moment

Then suddenly I was possessed by the reflex of a
   lesson learned too well
(An old lesson): that touches blow your cover
Only touch the one you *know* to be your lover

So I panicked. I stiffened. I jerked away.

And in the aching fierceness of the moment
Her very black eyes burned into mine

And I knew that that aborted embrace
Negated all we'd shared
But I was locked in silent shock, and she walked
    away forever

Oh Rosalind, what kind of world is this
That twists and tears our mightiest moment
That forces me to forsake our struggle for another
    left unspoken
That surely makes you see my act only as a
    last betrayal
That makes me assume that I was alone
In the fear
    at being
        queer.

    This is a story about how our histories and our experiences of oppression inform how we see things. Michelle and Linda heard this song and were angry. They felt wounded by it. They called it a racist song. They thought describing Rosalind's laugh as "husky and hearty" was a stereotypical way of describing Black women's laughter. They heard what sounded like a banjo at one point in the song and felt it was an improper appropriation of an African instrument. Meg tried to defend herself without being defensive. "But," she said, "Rosalind's laugh *was* deep—it *was* husky and hearty. Should I not say that because it's also stereotypical?" As to the banjo sound—there was no banjo on the record, but what they heard was a traditional Southern Appalachian picking style used for guitars and banjos. Meg said she had consciously chosen that style to represent the South because the story took place in the South, and Southern culture and traditions played a big role in it. This explanation infuriated Michelle, who thought Meg was glamorizing Southern culture, while, to Meg, having grown up there, it meant something quite different.

Michelle and Linda raised the question of whether the song should be pulled from the album, even though it had already been recorded and mixed. The discussion was filled with long silences. All of the white women, except Meg, either stayed silent or supported Michelle and Linda's position. Even though I didn't really understand the depth of their objections, I didn't know how to ask questions about it. I was afraid that to even raise a question would be seen as a racist act, and I didn't want to be seen as racist. I wanted to know whether it was ever okay to mention a stereotypical characteristic if the stereotype were true. What if there was a blonde who was dumb? A Jew who was pushy? An Irishman who was drunk? And what was the history behind Black women's voices being called "husky" that made it derogatory? I assumed it was something I should have already known about, and so I was afraid to ask.

In the end, we decided that it was too late to pull the song from the album (remember, when we made vinyl albums, there were two sides that had to be of roughly equal length). But we thought that Meg should not perform the song any more. Meg left the meeting and went to her room. I followed her after a bit. I felt so conflicted about the whole thing. I wanted to comfort her and didn't know how. I also wanted to be on the side of the women of color. It didn't occur to me that it was possible to do both.

The song was written almost like a mini-opera; there is no verse/chorus/verse. It just unfolds rather dramatically. It's a song about a friendship that is damaged both by racism and by internalized homophobia. In our meeting, we never talked about the latter and what an important part of the song it was. The pain in the song, for both women, is palpable. I can't say whether it's a good song. But I think it was a brave song. I think that Meg took a risk with both the music and the lyrics. What is most striking to me now is how hard it was to have a good conversation. Linda and Michelle were hurt and angry. Meg felt beaten up. I felt scared and confused. Everything was so much bigger than just a conversation about a couple of lines in a song. I wanted to accept leadership from the Black women, but in this case they didn't even all agree with each other. (Mary stayed quiet through this whole meeting, and later told me that she had no problem with Meg's song.) I imagine when the meeting was over we *all* felt pretty awful.

This was not the first, nor would it be the last time that we tried to address differences among us that showed up along race lines. Linda, Mary, and Michelle felt like they were already taking big risks to ally themselves so closely with white women—how far could they trust us to understand and deal with their everyday experiences of racism? What kinds of pressures were they feeling from their Black friends who were straight or male? But to everyone's credit, we kept at it. No matter how hard the conversations got, we all stayed at the table. Nobody walked out. We kept trying. All of us. We kept moving.

In 1977 alone, we produced and released four new albums—Teresa's *The Ways a Woman Can Be* (LF 910); *Lesbian Concentrate* (LF 915); Meg's second album (with "Rosalind"), *Face the Music* (LF 913); and *Linda Tillery* (BLF 917). (Linda wanted the B for Black inserted before our standard album coding of LF for Lesbian Feminist). To launch Linda's album, we produced the Entertainment Extravaganza that I wrote about in the prologue, with short sets by Meg, Teresa, Cris, and Pat Parker, and a full set by Linda and her band. We sold out two nights at the Oakland Auditorium—a total of four thousand tickets. While it made no sense musically (Linda later told me it was

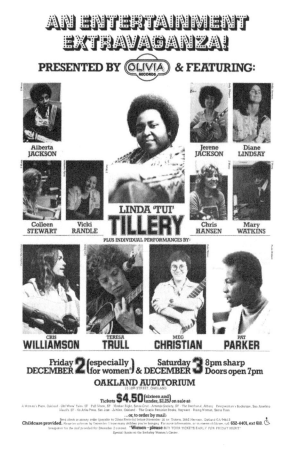

The poster for the Entertainment Extravaganza
we produced to launch *Linda Tillery*

like putting James Taylor and James Brown on the same bill
because their names were both James), the idea was to bring in
all the fans of each of these women to introduce them to all the
others. Most particularly, we wanted to use our big draws—Cris
and Meg—to bring women to Teresa and, especially, to Linda.
We still believed that the category of Women's Music, the Olivia

Records brand, would transcend genres and styles and personal taste. Sad to say, it did not turn out that way.

Our collective had grown and so had our catalog. Besides Olivia's records, we were distributing several albums by women artists who were recording on their own labels. We had two by the Berkeley Women's Music Collective, Kay Gardner's *Mooncircles*, a comedy album by Robin Tyler, and six others including a live album that Cris and her partner Jackie Robbins put together. (We didn't think the recording quality was good enough to be an Olivia record, so Cris and Jackie put it out on their own label and asked us to distribute it.)

We were thinking big about 1978—we had plans to record Mary Watkins and another studio album with Cris. I had been to New York in the fall of 1976 and seen Ntozake Shange's choreopoem *for colored girls who have considered suicide / when the rainbow is enuf* on Broadway. I immediately thought this would be a perfect project for Olivia to record and was disappointed to learn that there was already an original cast recording. But I began a correspondence with Ntozake, who was intrigued by Olivia and interested in working with us. We were unable to work out a recording arrangement, but, in 1979, we did produce her at the Oakland Auditorium in a concert with Mary Watkins. During this time, we approached Vicki Randle about doing an album, but she said she was not ready. And, with the popularity of Gwen Avery's rendition of "Sugar Mama" on *Lesbian Concentrate*, we began talking about getting Gwen in the studio for a full album.

To top it off, we started plotting what would become the Varied Voices of Black Women tour in 1978, with Linda, Mary, Gwen, and Pat Parker. The accompanying band was made up of both Black and white women, among them Vicki Randle on supporting vocals. Mary played piano for Linda, and Linda played drums for Mary and herself. They did a series of concerts on the West Coast, and we were disappointed by the low turnout of women of color. Consequently we contracted with Roadwork—a Washington, DC, company of women who produced concerts and booked tours for Sweet Honey in the Rock, among others—to book and coordinate the East Coast tour in November. We decided that, if we wanted to reach new audiences, having new artists might not be enough. So, where we could, we would work with women of color as producers, even though it might mean bypassing white or majority-white women's production companies who had supported us in the past. Our top priority was getting this show in front of women of color.

Roadwork wanted to get the show into Boston. Their main contact, like ours, was Artemis Productions, a predominantly white women's group. As we so often did, when what we wanted didn't exist yet, we made it up. We didn't know a Black women's production company in Boston, but we knew Black women. The Combahee River Collective was a trailblazing group of radical Black feminists formed in 1974, centered in Boston. In addition to their political activism, these women authored the "Combahee River Collective Statement," which still stands as one of the most sophisticated analyses of the intersections of racism and sexism. One of their members was Barbara Smith, who was two years behind me at Mount Holyoke College. Barbara and I had stayed in touch over the years, connected by our radicalism and feminism and lesbianism. So when we wanted to find a Boston producer, I called Barbara and asked her if she thought Combahee could put something together for the Varied Voices tour. The answer was a resounding "yes."

Boston was a small town, and the Combahee and Artemis women had worked together on previous projects. Together, they formed the Bessie Smith Memorial Production Collective for the express purpose of bringing this show to Boston. They

Promo flyer for the Mary Watkins/Ntozake Shange concert we produced

put on two shows at Boston University's Morse Auditorium, each selling out the 750-seat hall, and they brought the show to the women's prison in Framingham, about an hour outside of Boston.

In a recent conversation, Barbara told me how important it was to them to locate the concerts in a continuum of authentic African American cultural expression. Naming themselves after Bessie Smith was not random. At the concerts themselves, everyone in the audience received a fan—a reference to the fans passed out at Black churches—and these had an original graphic designed to look like African masks.

Most of the audiences were still majority-white, but women of color in general and Black women (and some men) in particular attended in great numbers. The two concerts in New York, plus the one in DC and the one at Rutgers in New Jersey had audiences that were mostly people of color.

The concerts were terrific—there were fourteen in all— and the audience response was pretty much over the top. A stage filled with African American women, each at the top of her game, performing material that was political and sensual, rock-inflected, jazz-based, and bluesy sexy. This was really an amazing and astounding collaboration. One of the highlights came when Linda, Mary, Vicki, and Gwen joined Pat on stage for a reading of Pat's stunning *Movement in Black*. Another came when Linda and the band performed "Freedom Time," a song that she and Mary had written. The song starts slowly and softly with what sounds like a lament from Linda that lasts for almost two minutes. It then moves into a jazz funk rhythm that leaves no doubt that this song is a call to action:

> No more prayin'
> No more cryin'
> Look all around you
> People are starvin' and dyin'
> Time for livin'

If you're willin'
It's freedom time, yeah

.....

If I could just tell you what it's really like
To live this life of triple jeopardy
I fight the daily battles of all my people
Just to sacrifice my pride and deny my strength

No more crying
No more weeping
'Cause I believe that I do hold up half the sky

Tell your children
Sister soldier
To have faith in
All of the things that you've told them
They'll believe you
Because they'll need you
At freedom time

Linda later told Joseph Beam in an interview in *Blacklight* that the Varied Voices tour "was the first time that a group of us were able to go and present ourselves as we truly are—four Black women, doing what we do, having people listen to it, and try to understand what that's about."

So many great things happened on this tour. But Gwen's alcohol consumption had become a serious problem. Though she was not the only woman who was drinking heavily, her resulting behavior was the most disruptive. Judy accompanied the group as road manager, and she said she struggled almost every night to get Gwen to the concert venue on time. And there were times when the struggle turned nasty. On stage, Gwen became a different person—happy and energetic and sexy—and she got audiences roaring with joy. But by the time the tour was over, Judy, Linda, and Mary had serious doubts about working with Gwen. As a result, after a lengthy discussion at one of our regular meetings, we canceled our plans to make a record with Gwen. Though Linda thought that, if Gwen did make a record, it could be very successful, Gwen had very little studio experience and would need a strong producer to help and guide her and to work around her erratic behavior. No one in the collective was willing to take that on.

Meanwhile, Olivia was struggling harder than ever. *Changer* continued to sell very well, and some of our other albums were doing reasonably well, but some were not. Our artists were on the road a lot and audiences were growing, but women had so many more choices now. Where once there had been three or five albums of Women's Music, now there were dozens. We had been hurt financially as well as spiritually by the backlash against our hiring of Sandy Stone. We were still dreaming of having our own studio. But we were spending money much faster than we were making it, and more and more of our meeting time and planning time was devoted to how to get ourselves out of a growing financial hole.

In the late fall of 1977, after our move north, we decided we needed to step back and take a big-picture look at what we were doing and how we were doing. I don't think I knew the term "white culture," but I did still firmly believe that how we did things would probably change in ways that were uncomfortable for me if we were truly going to be a multicultural organization. I'm pretty sure I didn't know what that really meant. At one meeting, we were outlining Olivia's goals, beginning with using feminist business as a means toward building a mass movement of women. This was one of the cornerstones of the original vision—that a business operating on feminist principles would add an economic component to the political and spiritual characterizations of feminism; that hundreds (maybe thousands) of jobs would be created to support the production of the music; that networks of distributors and concert producers would cover the country and use the music to organize women in every community; and that our ability to get the music into record stores and clubs and concert halls would ultimately get the music into the hearts of women everywhere.

So when Linda said very pointedly, "I feel pretty out of touch with that as a serious goal," I was taken aback. Looking back now, I can think of many reasons she might have said this. Perhaps she doubted that a feminist business could ever be that powerful. She certainly knew much more about how the music industry operated than any of the rest of us, and she might have questioned our ability to move masses of women with a few records. Whatever the reason, she certainly had an idea of our potential that was more grounded in reality than mine was. And her raising the issue led to more difficult, and unresolved, discussions.

Regardless of what Linda meant in that moment of that meeting about that goal, it was clear that she was not as comfortable declaring women-only space as I was, or as the other original collective members were. Nor was Mary. Nor was Cris, for that matter, but Cris was not a member of the collective, so while her resistance was frustrating to me, it wasn't more than that. But Linda and Mary were full collective members and their challenge to this core belief about women-only space was unnerving for me.

Recalling the line from "Freedom Time"—"If I could just tell you what it's really like / To live this life of triple jeopardy"—I didn't fully understand the struggles that black lesbians faced (and still face). I had a deep and very personal understanding of homophobia, misogyny, and sexism. My understanding of racism was pretty intellectual and largely limited to the kinds

238 | Ginny Z Berson

of overt acts that were giving way to more subtle expressions, which, in some ways, were more damaging for being so insidious. And I did not understand the particular pressure that Black lesbians felt from other African Americans who thought that issues around gender and sexuality should be subordinated to racial solidarity.

Linda and Mary—like all the Olivia musicians—continued to perform occasionally at women-only concerts and continued to use only women musicians for Olivia-produced records and concerts. But the issue festered, and continued to raise questions for me about how to recognize which of our policies and practices were a product of our whiteness and would have to change if we were really going to be the multiracial, multicultural organization—and movement—that I dreamed of. I found it much easier to let go of a lot of the "how" we did things, but I wasn't sure I was willing to let go of the "why"—our vision, our core beliefs and our values.

By the end of 1979, Linda and several other women had left the collective—mostly for financial reasons, and I was thinking about leaving too. But for Linda and others, leaving Olivia did not mean leaving behind the contradictions. In the spring of 1980, she was hired to perform for the National Women in the Law Conference in Oakland. She put together a band that included Mary on keyboards, several other women instrumentalists, and supporting vocalists. The guitarist was the highly regarded Ray Obiedo, an African American man. At least some of the promotional material for the concert listed the band members, including Ray. Knowing this, some women came to the concert with the intent to disrupt. They brought raw eggs, and, when the band took the stage, they threw those eggs at Linda and the band. There were gasps from the audience, Linda gave them the finger from the stage, the egg-throwers were escorted out, and the band played on. (Later, some women expressed outrage that they hadn't been told in advance that a man would be on stage, claiming they wouldn't have bought tickets had they known. But clearly some women knew about the men, unless they always brought bags full of raw eggs with them to concerts.)

I was disgusted by the egg-throwers and furious at them—at their so-called purity, their ignorance of who Linda was, their expectations that she was "theirs." I remember thinking to myself, "How can anyone think this is feminism? Is this what I'm supposed to be fighting for?"

For the next few months, the feminist media was filled with commentary about the concert—not the egg-throwing, but the man on the stage. One letter-writer called it "a raw wound in the breast of the women's community." Thankfully, many women rose to Linda's defense and tried to talk about how African American women just might have different needs and issues and desires for connection than white women.

But this incident, this behavior, was reminiscent of Slimy Sunday—lesbian feminist women venting their rage on other lesbian feminist women for not reflecting back a perfect mirror image. I had seen the poster, and I knew that Ray would be playing with Linda. I was disappointed that she was choosing to work with a man because I wanted her to want the same things I wanted. But at the same time, I was beginning to understand that there was nothing revolutionary or feminist about that stance.

One by one, Linda, Mary, and Michelle left Olivia, each for her own reasons. Although race differences were never explicitly given as a reason for anyone's leaving, it is impossible to say that they were not a part of anyone's reasons. Race was not a simple, single thread that could be separated out and pulled from the whole fabric of the Olivia experience.

Those of us who remained continued to struggle with these questions of how to achieve the largeness of our vision, to be more inclusive of all women, while still working only with women, some of whom had important ties to men. But at a certain point, these issues became moot because we had such serious financial problems that we had to shrink the collective and shrink the business. Our focus moved to survival.

21 FACE THE MUSIC
The Crash

I N THE BEGINNING WAS THE music, and as I've said, I thought the music was so magical and so powerful that if we could just get access to the hearts of women, the revolution would be assured. Millions of women would embrace feminism, come out as lesbians, and throw off the remaining bonds of patriarchy. We would fire no guns. We would just, little by little, create a world that worked for all of us, and women would see what we were doing and want to be part of it and bring their own ideas of how to make it even better and, together, we would. All we had to do was get the music heard. All we had to do was get our music on the radio. I admit that this was not a highly developed plan, but I was in love with this idea of a women's record company, and I was in love with Meg, and this was not a dreamy dream, a head-in-the-clouds dream, this was a feet-on-the-ground, fire-in-the-belly dream.

Unfortunately, getting airplay on the hit-making commercial radio stations was about as hard as getting a lesbian feminist elected president of the United States. Before music videos and digital music, getting into heavy rotation on key radio stations in key markets—especially LA and New York—was the ticket to selling records. Most music stations were independently owned. The era of the giant chains and networks had not yet arrived. Stations reported what they were playing to industry journals like *Billboard*, and, if a song was getting a lot of play on a top LA station, for example, stations all over the country would add it to their playlist. This was such a critical piece of the profit-making puzzle for record labels that bribing DJs—the original "pay to play" was fairly common. This practice was called "payola," and it was uncovered and outlawed in the early 1960s. (But even as late as the early 2000s, the practice was still going on. In 2005, executives at Sony BMG labels admitted that they had made deals with several large commercial radio chains, and they paid a $10 million fine.) In order to preempt individual DJs from making deals with record promoters, a lot of radio stations instituted playlists which were created by the program director or music director. DJs were required to choose the music they played from these predetermined playlists. This made it easier, in one sense, and harder in another, for an independent label or a random song to get on the air. Easier because instead of having to approach every DJ at key stations, promo people only had to approach a few program directors. Harder because there was no chance that a DJ might hear something he liked (and they were almost all men) and give it a spin.

Try as we might, until Linda Tillery's album came out, almost all the airplay we got was on grassroots community radio stations. These stations were popping up all over the country in the 1970s, and their programming reflected the identity politics of the time. Most, if not all of them, had at least one "women's" show that played Women's Music, and our records were on all of them. Our touring artists were always invited in for interviews before their concerts. This was a terrific source of free publicity for us, and introduced our music to lots of women, but the audiences for these programs and stations were small, and they did not have the reach of the commercial stations. Linda's album, and later Mary's, did get some play on some commercial stations, but they were never in heavy rotation—never among the songs that got the most airplay—and the records themselves were not always readily available in the mainstream record stores, so the airplay didn't result in the kind of breakthrough sales we were hoping for.

But we kept trying. We hired a male professional record promoter to call radio stations and try to get them to listen and add songs from our records to their playlists. We also tried magical thinking—Sandy Stone made signs that she hung over everyone's desks in the office that said "Think Airplay!" Desperate times call for desperate measures. And we were starting to get desperate.

Another way to draw attention to our music was by getting prominent reviewers to write about the records or concerts. There was a time in our very early days when we demanded that reviewers and interviewers be female, and, if the magazine or newspaper didn't have any women on staff, too bad for them. This worked at least once, when a newspaper hired a female photographer to accompany the female reporter because of our insistence, but for the most part the media needed our story less than we needed the publicity, and we had to let that idea go. We identified some influential music critics in LA and sent them promo copies of all our records, invited them to every local concert, over and over again, and for the most part they ignored us. Then Cris had a gig at McCabe's, which was a small but important club in Santa Monica, and, lo and behold, one of the top critics for the *LA Times* came to the show and wrote a glowing review, which started with a reproach to Olivia for trying to keep Cris's talent a secret. This was the kind of arrogant ignorance that drove me crazy.

The distribution network had grown in convoluted and contradictory ways. There were a few women who were serious about building their own businesses, and to do this they

244 | Ginny Z Berson

needed more territory—which meant giving up our idea of a distributor-who-was-really-a-community-organizer in every town. It meant we had to let go of our anger at the other labels who hooked into the network without any acknowledgement that Olivia had built it. It meant letting go of the idea that the distribution network was Olivia's. At the same time, we had a number of distributors who, for one reason or another, seemed to lose their interest in Women's Music. Some of them kept fairly large inventories on hand that they weren't selling and wouldn't return to us. Some of them sold their inventories and stopped sending us the money they collected from stores and other sales. One woman later told me that she had used the money she owed us to help pay for her first year of law school. She said she had never liked the financial arrangements Olivia had with distributors (although she signed up to be a distributor with full knowledge of the terms), and so she thought it was fine for her to keep all the money. We certainly didn't want to take anyone to court, but we were having very bad cash flow problems, and we needed to do something. We ended up asking our lawyer to write slightly threatening letters to a few women, and in some cases we were able to work out payment terms with them. In other cases, we just had to write off these bad debts.

With financial pressures growing, we began to consider new strategies. Jennifer got dressed up and went to speak with a loan officer at the bank where we had our accounts. The loan application was denied. We looked into finding investors and forming a limited partnership, but decided the legal and financial requirements were too onerous for us to consider, plus we didn't know where we would find women with the kind of money we needed. Liza Williams, our promotion person, suggested that we record Mary and try to get a major jazz label to take on the distribution. We decided not to do that because, even if we could make such an arrangement, the amount of money that would come to us would hardly pay our production costs. We couldn't figure out what to do, and we were getting into a bigger and bigger hole. We owed money to everyone. We recorded Mary's album, *Something Moving*, in the summer of 1978, hoping to have it on hand for the Varied Voices tour. At that point, we had a big order at the pressing plant we used. We were almost out of Cris's *The Changer and the Changed*—still our biggest seller—and were running low on several other titles as well. We needed to stock up for holiday sales, which we hoped would keep us afloat. We kept expecting a big shipment of records, and the big shipment kept not arriving. Finally somebody called the pressing plant, and we were told that they were not going to press or ship us any more records until we paid our bill. Our bill was enormous. Many thousands of dollars. We were screwed. If we couldn't press records, we couldn't sell records, and so we would never have the money to pay the presser.

Liz Brown had taken over all the bookkeeping for Olivia, and one morning in October she called us together. "I have an idea," she said with her soft North Carolina twang. "I tried to think about what I do when a distributor or a store owes us a lot of money and can't pay. So I want to offer the pressing plant a deal. We will pay cash for all the new pressings we need and commit to a regular payment schedule to pay off our debt. If they go for this, we'll have *Changer* for Christmas, plus get Mary's album, plus have stock for everything else." A simple and brilliant idea that gave us a tiny ray of hope.

Jennifer, Michelle, and Liz, our financial team, went off to figure out how much we could offer them towards paying off the debt and how to frame the conversation. They made the phone call and we all held our breath. The owner of the pressing plant agreed. He promised us that records would arrive within the week. We were saved.

But we were hardly safe. By 1978, we had grown way beyond a seat-of-the-pants, five-woman collective operation to a full-fledged business, and the total amount of business education all of us had was that couple of weeks at the New School. We were learning as much as we could as quickly as we could, trying to operate in a financially responsible and sustainable way, while still clinging to our socialist principles. We had to let Sandy Stone and Liza Williams go. We couldn't afford to keep an engineer on staff when we didn't have enough money to make any records. Liza wanted and needed more money than we could pay her, and, although she wrote lively and sexy copy, we felt we had to spend our minuscule publicity and marketing budget on people whose expertise and focus was on getting airplay.

But losing these two women was not enough. We needed help. When Judy was back east with the Varied Voices tour, she heard about Women's Resources, a business consulting company run by two lesbians—Evie Litwok and Rose Weber. We agreed to hire them, and they came out to Oakland in early 1979. They studied our books; they sat in on our meetings; they met with us as individuals. They asked a million questions and then they suggested a plan of action designed to get us out of debt and back to doing the work we wanted to do. The biggest item on their list was that we had to reduce our payroll. We simply could not afford to support what were now twelve women. Robin, who had become my dear friend and ran the distribution network with me, saw the writing on the wall. Even before the Women's Resource plan, she announced that she would be leaving. Mary was next—she later told me that she felt that she was pushed out, but that, in fact, it had turned out well for her. She said she was starting to feel like a drag on the collective, and she also wanted to be able to grow musically in ways that she didn't think Olivia could support.

Linda left voluntarily because she also wanted to do more than either she or Olivia felt comfortable with, and she also wanted to be able to make more money than we could afford. It seemed unlikely that there would be another Olivia album in her immediate future; her opportunities to produce others were limited because we weren't producing others, and there were a few male musicians she wanted to work with. Michelle had pretty much stopped coming to work altogether, and she was asked to leave. That left Jennifer, Kate, Teresa, Meg, Liz, Judy, Sandy Ramsey, and me.

Jennifer and Liz oversaw the business parts of the business. Judy was doing some of the business, keeping on top of pressings, and booking some tours. Teresa and Meg continued to tour and deal with all the tapes we got from musicians wanting to be recorded by Olivia. Sandy Ramsey was the office manager and ran all the packing and shipping. Kate still did whatever graphic design and layout we needed and helped Sandy Ramsey ship out record orders. I ran the distribution network, worked with the other labels whose records we were distributing, and produced Olivia's concert series, which was an important source of income. But, once again, we were an all-white collective. This was depressing.

And there was more. To the extent that we still had them, we had to abandon the idea of a distributor in every town. We had to allow and encourage consolidation among the really successful distributors and revisit the idea of using male-owned one-stops, or regional record distribution centers. If we wanted to produce an album in 1979—and we very much wanted to get a new studio album done by Cris—we would have to fundraise for it.

We sent a letter to our extensive mailing list. We began by saying, "We're writing to you because we need your help." After quickly running through a little Olivia history, we explained the nature of our predicament.

> Desiring to extend decision-making to a broader group of women, but lacking the sophisticated business skills to evaluate how many women we could adequately support, we expanded our group faster that we could afford to. Wishing to broaden the scope of the women's music we record, we produced albums by very talented lesser-known artists; but without the funds to tour these artists and promote their albums, we have not always succeeded in making the excellence of their music known to women around the country. The consequences—combined with the handicap of inflation and recession we all face today—have been severe for Olivia. We have had to cut back staff; we are operating with a sizable deficit; we have been unable to produce a new album this year.
>
> Now Olivia is at a crossroads—and once again we turn to you for support.

We said we had an opportunity to produce an album that people would love as much as they had loved *Changer*, an album we were sure would be an enormous help in getting us out of debt. We said we needed to raise $40,000 to make it happen. And we asked people to support us by buying records from our catalog (order blank enclosed with the letter), make a donation, or contact us if they could make a loan of $1,000 or more. We closed by saying, "We want you to know that Olivia isn't about to die." We expressed confidence that we would be able to release the new album and keep on.

The response was strong enough that we raised the $40,000 and released Cris Williamson's second studio album on the Olivia label, *Strange Paradise*, in March 1980.

So Olivia would go on. But I wasn't sure how much longer I would be a part of it. In November 1979, I started thinking seriously about leaving. I made a list of what I liked and didn't like about Olivia. The "like" list included "sense of accomplishment; be my own boss; no men; good pay; travel; can implement my ideas; no supervisor and nobody I supervise." The "don't like" list was a little shorter, but the items were a little weightier: "feel uninspired; lack of direction; lack of vision." It was becoming clear that the path we had chosen was not sustainable. We could not be a revolutionary political/cultural organization and a successful business. We could be one or the other, but, in our attempts to be both, we were failing at both. To keep the music flowing and feeding women individually and collectively, we needed to act more like a business. When I finally understood that, I knew I would leave. If we couldn't run the business based on feminist principles, I didn't see the point. For me, the business was always just a means to an end.

Once I made the decision to go, I was actually relieved. I had loved creating Olivia, doing every part of the work, helping to make the music that was helping to build the movement, sharing the excitement that women felt when they experienced a concert of Women's Music or listened to an Olivia record. I loved watching us grow. Every part of it was hard, but there was so much joy and love, and I was so convinced of the rightness of what we were doing that I was sure that we would succeed. Now, it seemed like nothing but struggle. I was still holding on to the vision, but I didn't see any way to get there. I was finished.

Jennifer was the first of the original collective to leave, in the spring of 1980. I stayed until August. When Judy bought out my "share" of Olivia for $3,500, I thought it was a ridiculously low amount, but I also knew that it was all Olivia could afford. And anyway, I hadn't ever been in it for the money.

Judy took over running the company, no longer a collective, and kept making records for another fifteen years. In the face of a rapidly changing industry, she managed to put out thirty-four more albums, including more by Meg, Cris, and Teresa, and new additions like Deidre McCalla. Judy also started a new label—Second Wave—which had mostly bands. Its featured musicians (Tret Fure, Diane Davidson, Alicia Bridges among them) were women and some of their side players were men. In November 1982, Judy and Olivia produced two sold-out shows at Carnegie Hall with Meg and Cris and an extraordinary all-woman band (Linda Tillery, Vicki Randle, Adrienne Torf, Tret Fure, Diane Lindsay, Judy Chilnick, Shelby Flint, Jackie Robbins, and Jeanette Wrate).

She launched the first cruise in 1990. Olivia is now a very successful lesbian travel company. Olivia Records is no more.

CHANGE

Epilogue

RONALD REAGAN WAS ELECTED PRESIDENT in 1980, and that effectively put an end to the era known as the Sixties—although much of the powerful political and cultural expression attributed to the Sixties happened in the Seventies. It's not that Richard Nixon, Gerald Ford, and Jimmy Carter had led progressive administrations, but with Reagan's ascension, the country swung way to the right. The already pathetic restraints on capitalism were further weakened, and greed was glamorized and glorified. "More, more, more" was the mantra of the day. The object of the "more" was money. And more was never enough.

We saw this in the music business as labels merged, and media companies expanded and bought out their competition. We saw it in the vertical integration of labels, concert promoters, and radio stations. If the corporation that owns the record label also owns the radio network, you don't need payola to get your records played. Record labels started dropping artists who were not hitting the top of the charts. Record stores started acting like real estate brokers, measuring success by how much money they took in per square foot. There was no room for slow- or low-selling records.

All of this preceded the complete upending of the music business when everything went digital, but that was later. At the time I left Olivia, in August 1980, after seven and a half years, the force we were facing, and trying to either get around or subvert, was enormous and beyond our capacity to impact. Olivia Records kept on, although it no longer operated as a collective. By 1984, everyone had left but Judy, and all the women she hired to help were employees, not decision-makers.

A few of the women left with some anger or bitterness directed at the collective or an individual in the collective or the women's movement or the super-separatists or the other women's labels or our inability to meet our goals. What is amazing to me now is that we functioned together as well as we did for as long as we did. We had to struggle through our political disagreements and our varying degrees of consciousness and commitment. And we didn't all necessarily like each other particularly or equally. You will be shocked to learn that some of us had irritating habits! We weren't always nice to each other. Some of us yelled at others. Plus, many of us had serious or casual sex with each other, and sometimes it was both. Couples came together and broke up. In spite of whatever sexual tension there was, in spite of practically living on top of each other at different points, and working together, and sitting in endless meetings with each other, we hung in with each other. We were almost always able to put aside our personal feelings—for better or worse—because the Work meant so much.

The ways that life changed for lesbians and women in the next forty years were astonishing. When I wrote the first draft of this book, Hillary Clinton had just been nominated as the candidate of the Democratic Party for President of the United States. As far as she was from being a feminist candidate, it was an extraordinary accomplishment. At the same time, the relentlessness of the misogynistic vitriol that was heaped on her was disgusting and horrifying. And we all know who won the election. Sexism and misogyny were surely a huge part of it. Sexism and misogyny are alive and well, among the Left as well as the Right, among women as well as men.

Olivia Records did not get Hillary Clinton nominated. We did not lead the charge for marriage equality or anti-discrimination laws or Title IX or the right to serve in the military or the higher consciousness around domestic violence, rape, pay equity, reproductive freedom, or the myriad other issues that have been brought to the fore since the 1970s. Olivia Records didn't even change the music business very much, although now it's not so unusual to see women on stage with their instruments—like Regina Carter and her jazz violin, Bonnie Raitt and her slide guitar, Laurie Anderson and her electronics, Anoushka Shankar and her sitar, Sheila E. and her drums. Women are producing and engineering music. Women are writing and performing songs with feminist content in every genre—like Janelle Monáe, Hurray for the Riff Raff, Ani DiFranco (who started her own label—Righteous Babe), Lizzo, Toshi Reagon, Alicia Keys, Dar Williams, Jill Scott, Tracy Chapman, and Austra. Olivia Records did not do any of these things. What we did was throw a small stone in the water and make a little splash. And the ripples are still expanding.

We produced music that changed people's lives, that made women feel stronger, that helped them heal, that raised their consciousness, that celebrated their loves and their lives. We helped women feel connected to something bigger than themselves. We helped create community. We helped women get in touch with their own personal power and the power that comes from joining with others to make change. We taught women skills that helped them get jobs and form networks that helped other women feel connected, learn skills, get jobs, and on and on.

We did not do this alone. We were part of a movement that created and produced: books and bookstores, newspapers and radio shows, coffee houses and restaurants, battered women's shelters and rape crisis centers, foundations and new fundraising models, political organizations and land trusts. This movement invented new ways to do therapy and new ways to do music festivals, new ways to write poetry and new ways to experience and express spirit.

Like the Reaganites of the '80s, the mantra of our movement was also "more, more, more," but it was never about money. We wanted—and still want—more justice, more equity, more freedom.

Regardless of the labels women use today to identify themselves as being engaged in the struggle for liberation—understanding that unless *all women* are liberated no one will be liberated—that struggle goes on. Some of the actions women take to lead and participate in movements for change are more risky, and yet they take them. The times are so different now, and so are and must be the responses. Every generation has its own dreams for its own future. Undoubtedly, today's activists will not hold the same dreams in the same way that we held ours, and that's as it should be. What I hope is that people will look at what we did and tried to do, where we succeeded and where we failed, and learn from it. I hope that today's women will not make the same mistakes we made—there are so many new mistakes to be made! I hope that today's women will bring fresh eyes and ideas to the questions that confounded us and invent new solutions, or, if not solutions, new paths forward. Most of all, I hope that all of us can learn how to come to this work with love. That we make a conscious commitment to treat each other with respect and compassion. That we bring curiosity rather than judgment to people not like us. That our process—*how* we do everything—reflects the outcomes we want. That we act as if every single thing we do represents the world we want to live in, that our values are not something to be achieved later, but something to be lived now.

Today, I still would not be allowed to play baseball in the Major Leagues, but I could play Little League, and I could get a softball scholarship for college, and I could play in the Olympics. That seems like something.

The truth is, given what we were up against, we didn't have a chance. And yet we changed the world.

Timeline

1971   Furies collective forms

Jan. 1972   First issue of *The Furies* published

Fall 1972   Last issue of *The Furies* by the original collective published

March 1972   Meg and Ginny become lovers

1972   Furies collective disbands

May–June 1973   Last issue of *The Furies* published

Jan. 1973   First meeting of the group that would become Olivia Records

Spring 1973   Cris pops the question: "Why don't you start a women's record company?"

Summer 1973   Meg and Ginny drive to West Coast, meet Margie Adam, Vicki Randle, and Joan Lowe

1974   Olivia records and releases 45 rpm (*Lady* and *If It Weren't for the Music*)

Fall 1974 Olivia and Meg's first album, *I Know You Know,* recorded

March 1975 Olivia collective moves to LA. *I Know You Know* released

Fall 1975 Cris Williamson: *The Changer and the Changed*

Feb. 1976 Women on Wheels tour

1976 *BeBe K'Roche*

Where Would I Be Without You? The Poetry of Pat Parker and Judy Grahn

Dec. 1976 Slimy Sunday

1977 Teresa Trull: *The Ways a Woman Can Be*

Meg Christian: *Face the Music*

Lesbian Concentrate

Olivia moves to the Bay Area

Linda Tillery

1978 Mary Watkins: *Something Moving*

1978 Varied Voices of Black Women tour

1980 Cris Williamson: *Strange Paradise*